BOOKS ARE FOR PEOPLE

A LIBRARIAN'S LIFE

Other books in the MY LIFE AND MY WORK series:

MY LIFE AND MY WORK SERIES

Books are for People

A Librarian's Life

James Dearden, FLA

with a Foreword by Dr. George Chandler, MA, FLA, FRHistS

EDUCATIONAL EXPLORERS LIMITED · READING

First published 1969
© James A. Dearden 1969
SBN 85225 725 2X

Published by Educational Explorers Limited
40 Silver Street, Reading, England
Set in 'Monotype' Bembo and printed in Great Britain by
Lamport Gilbert Printers Limited, Reading

CONTENTS

ACKNOWLEDGEMENT

The Author and Publisher gratefully acknowledge the kind help and advice given by the Library Association and Mr Bernard Palmer; and are indebted to them for providing a number of photographs for illustrations. These are published by kind permission of the copyright owners mentioned in the Author's Preface.

ILLUSTRATIONS

Inset between pages 52 and 53

PREFACE

BOOKS ARE NOT made by authors alone. This is my story, but it would not have been told without the kind thought of Mr A. C. Jones who first suggested to my publisher that I should write it.

Once I had embarked upon the narrative, my task was made easier by the generous assistance of three people, and I record their help and my gratitude with pleasure. Miss Dorothy Harrop cheerfully deciphered my manuscript and, through her comments, made sure that I kept professionally to the rails. Without my wife and her constant encouragement much of the story might never have happened, and both she and my daughter, Heather, provided valuable assistance at the typing and proof-reading stages.

The illustrations have not been chosen specifically to chart my path through librarianship, but rather to offer as broad a view as possible of what our work entails. Pictures often speak louder than words, and for their kindness in allowing me to reproduce their photographs I am most grateful to the following copyright owners:

Illustration 1: Mr K. A. Stockham, Nottinghamshire County Library, and Raymond's News Agency; 2: Mr D. I. Colley, and the Manchester Public Libraries; 3: Mr R. Hall, and the John Rylands Library; 4: Mr K. Carter, Dorset County Library and Herbert of Weymouth; 5 & 13: Mr P. D. Friend G.M., and the Atomic Weapons Research Establishment Library; 6: Mr J. Thompson, and Reading University Library; 7 to 10, 12, 15, 16 and jacket photograph: Mr W. R. Maidment, the Libraries, Arts & Amenities Committee of the London Borough of Camden, Photonews Ltd, and the North London Press; 14: Miss E. M. T. Markwick, and the Gloucestershire County Council; 11, 17 & 18: The British Council, the Central Office of Information and the *Welwyn Times*.

JAMES DEARDEN

College of Librarianship Wales,
Aberystwyth,
Cardiganshire.

FOREWORD

by

GEORGE CHANDLER, MA, PhD, FLA, FRHistS

I CONGRATULATE THE publishers on the excellent idea of publishing a series of volumes on *My Life and My Work*. Certainly, these books will not only help school leavers to decide whether they are likely to be attracted to a particular profession, but will also be of general interest.

Mr. Dearden was an excellent choice to write on librarianship because he has had interesting experiences in a number of different types of libraries, including a research library, special libraries, college libraries and branch public libraries, culminating in his present post as Lecturer at a School of Librarianship.

Mr. Dearden writes interestingly and well about his experiences, and few librarians can have had a wider range. Nevertheless, it is impossible for any single librarian to have had experience of all aspects of librarianship. There are, for instance, increasing opportunities for international work in librarianship. Many library associations throughout the world have international relations committees and there are many opportunities for overseas service in developing countries and with international organisations.

Even if librarians are not able actually to work overseas, international contacts are becoming increasingly necessary through international conferences, working parties and study groups. As a result of the spread of further education and industry, the peoples of the world need increasingly to have information on overseas countries and they turn to their libraries for assistance. In order to meet these demands, international library collaboration has grown rapidly during the last few years and will continue to increase in the future.

I hope that Mr. Dearden's excellent personal account of his work as a librarian will help others to appreciate more fully the value of the work which librarians are carrying out throughout the world.

I

INTRODUCTION

Friends who see me at work readily agree that I have an interesting profession, but nevertheless they are still liable to ask, 'What do you do *all day*? Don't you get bored among all those books? Some of them are as dry as dust'. And there is no short answer except to say what librarianship is not, for it is much much more than date-stamping books as they are borrowed, or charging a fine when an overdue loan is returned. Those are non-professional routine tasks usually carried out by library clerks.

A librarian's day is often full of the unexpected. A letter in the morning's mail has set me off on a two-hour search for a detailed perspective illustration of a rag-breaker used in paper-making. That was for an author preparing a new book in her retreat deep in the mountains. A telephone call proved to be a request for help from another librarian (sensibly, we help one another when the resources of our own library are exhausted). He needed information on soldering gold wire for use in missile components.

Then there was the lady who came into the library after listening to a radio programme. She asked for the Chinese poems of Wei Lee. After a little thought we realised that what she was really searching for were poems translated out of the Chinese by the famous scholar Arthur Waley. A grubby note in a child's hand requests a 'good book' for his mother, who is too busy to come to the library herself, and this can be just as difficult as some of the more technical queries, for she may not regard Tolstoy or Iris Murdoch as 'good' authors even if I do, and, when I have found what I think will be a suitable choice, how can I be sure that she has not read it before?

So librarians provide a service, selecting and collecting together books, journals and many other forms of record, audio as well as visual, and use their knowledge, skill and experience to make their stock easily available to their readers. To do this we also have to be good organisers, good personnel managers (for few of us work single-handed), prepared to be interested in all manner of subjects, and have a sincere liking for and understanding of people as well as books. The librarian who cannot mix with and talk to people he may never have seen before is at a grave disadvantage: he has to be able to study people so that he can help them properly. Given these essential qualities the top posts of our profession are open to both men and women.

Yet, after all that, I must admit that I became a librarian by accident. Towards the end of my schooldays I was only sure of one thing: I knew I did not want to go into a Bank or do any other sort of office work. Then, because I liked and was good at drawing I decided that I would be an architect, and my school arranged for me to be interviewed by one of Manchester's leading architects. Gently he pointed out that the building industry was in the doldrums owing to the Second World War —this was 1940—and he advised me to look for some other profession. Little did he know that the ground had been swept from under my feet and that I had not the slightest idea for an alternative. I hated the thought of clerical work, and I had no interest in the practical side of science and technology.

Fortunately my Headmaster had enough imagination for both of us after I had made my report of the interview. 'It just so happens', he said, 'that they want a trainee librarian at the John Rylands Library. You have worked in the school library' —I had, but had not thought of that as work because I liked it— 'so go and have a look. See whether you like them and they like you'. I went. I was fascinated. I was offered the post, and twenty-seven years later I still cannot think of any career I might have enjoyed more or pursued with greater success.

Today, of course, my Headmaster would have persuaded me to stay on at school for another two years, for the modern trainee librarian must have a minimum of two 'A' levels and three 'O' level passes in his G.C.E. before he can even start training, and a growing number of aspirants qualify professionally with a post-graduate course after extending their general education at university.

Also today, applicants are not expected to drop in for interview so naïvely as I did. They are expected to have had a long cool look at libraries before they arrive, to have made some appraisal of their local library service from the customer's point of view, and to have some awareness of the various types of library service that exist, for every librarian eventually becomes something of a specialist. One can serve in a general lending library or work only with children, catalogue and classify the stock behind the scenes, or work in a reference library—general or devoted to special topics—where all books must be used on the premises. Universities and colleges have their own types of library. So do government departments and the larger firms. There are even opportunities for foreign service with the British Council and the United Nations Organisation, for example.

2

TRAINEE AT THE JOHN RYLANDS LIBRARY

THE JOHN RYLANDS LIBRARY was a wonderful place in which to start my career. I only sensed it at the time of my interview, but the confirmation followed with each successive day I worked there. The library stands in the centre of Manchester flanked by shops and offices. It was built in the 1890's at the expense of his widow as a monument to a wealthy cotton merchant, and one must admit that it looks more like a church than anything else, so that the average passer-by is never quite sure as to its real function. But ask a scholar about the earliest known papyrus fragment of the New Testament or the St. Christopher block-print; and, whether you speak to him in America, Central Europe or Australia, he will know all about *The John Rylands*. Nobody bothers to add 'library'.

Starting at any new place of work is strange, but the first day of one's first job is the strangest experience of them all. At school I had been a member of one of the upper forms; now I was back at the bottom of the ladder, rather like a first-former knowing neither what to expect nor really what he ought to be doing. Everyone was very kind. I was introduced to the various members of the staff and given a guided tour of the collections, then left in the care of one of the more senior assistants to take up my duties at the counter.

Although the library still adds current publications to its stock, its primary importance stems from its special collections of manuscripts, early printed books, and fine bindings, the nucleus of which cost Mrs. Rylands some £500,000 in 1900.

There are clay tablets from Assyria and papyrus rolls by the yard from Egypt, that date back to the times of the Pharaohs.

From the monasteries of Europe there are service books all written and beautifully decorated by hand in reds, blues and gold leaf, as well as histories of the world as it then was. The printing of books from movable type, dates in Europe from the early 15th century, and examples at Rylands include the first printed Bible, produced at Mainz in Germany about 1455-56 (the so-called Gutenberg Bible), its paper stronger and whiter than some of today's book paper.

From 15th century London there are copies of Chaucer's tales printed near Westminster Abbey by the first English printer, William Caxton. When pocket books are mentioned today one automatically thinks of Penguins, but the first cheap editions small enough to fit into a student's pocket were printed in Venice in 1501. Rylands has almost a complete set of these Aldines, as they are called, after their originator, the scholar-printer Aldus Manutius.

Mr. Rylands was also an ardent church-goer so the library was well stocked with books on theology to reflect this interest, and practically all other subjects except science and technology were also strongly covered. In other words the John Rylands is an arts library for academics, and its readers are mostly final year undergraduates working on their theses, university lecturers and professors, and a sprinkling of the local clergy working up a sermon.

In such a library it is a normal rule that no item of stock may be removed from the premises. All the readers must carry out their researches within the library, and so they tend to become regular attenders, starting early in the morning and carrying on, with a break for lunch, until evening for months or even years at a stretch. To obtain an item from the stock the reader must first locate its presence in the catalogue, the key to the whole library. Then the details are entered on to a request slip which is

presented at the counter. The work of the junior assistants was
to receive these requests, fetch the item from one of the many
floors of the stacks and take it to the reader. With a stock of
over half a million items one has to know one's way around!

If a very rare item was required the request might need vetting
by a more senior member of the staff. For example, no raw junior
was allowed to fetch up papyrus fragments from the strong
rooms. Such trust was only extended to us after we had proved
unlikely to charge about or trip up, yet this 'promotion', when
it came, had its own snags. Papyrus is so brittle that it had been
sandwiched between sheets of plate glass to preserve it (perspex
had not been invented at that time). The strong rooms were in
the sub-basement, and between them and the lift was a stone-
paved corridor along which the glass had to be carried in one's
arms. Thus we quickly learned that any sort of promotion also
involves added responsibilities.

Such fetching and carrying may be considered a very menial
task hardly requiring a good G.C.E., and in many libraries now
it is done by unskilled labour. Nevertheless it did enable us to
get to know the stock at first hand. Thus we quickly learned the
existence and importance of works we had never even dreamed of.
Equally important we got to know our readers and their interests.
Librarianship is not an impersonal service: it is often a joint
effort locating through one's own experience, curiosity and
knowledge a piece of information which the reader hopes has
been recorded and which he in turn can use by the application
of his own special knowledge. The more searching one does, the
greater is the chance of success, for experience is priceless and
cuts down the number of false leads. One day the computer
may take over all such work, but that is still a long way off
except for the most straight-forward searching.

I always find the greatest trouble lies in the interesting by-
ways I discover and want to explore. Gradually an acquaintance
with all kinds of subjects is picked up and new paths of personal

reading followed because of curiosity and interest. All this does not make you an expert in everything, but it does make you a more interesting person while, at times, work seems closely akin to some intellectual parlour game on television for which, like those on TV, you also get paid.

Naturally, when little service to readers was required, this side of our work did not keep us fully occupied, and it was then that I was introduced to other tasks. A living library always has new additions that require to be catalogued and classified in order that their existence in the library may be made known to potential users. Often there are back-logs of this work if large numbers of volumes are unexpectedly donated. The procedures to be followed are of a very specialised nature, and some librarians will devote all their time to it because they find that their professional interests lie in that direction.

Even so, some of the more straightforward additions can be dealt with by less experienced staff so long as their work is checked by the full-time cataloguers, and these items came to us at the counter to be dealt with when things were quiet. In this way the cataloguers were able to concentrate on the more complicated works, but, more important, we juniors had the satisfaction of learning how to apply the rules of the cataloguing code and select suitable classification numbers from the Dewey Decimal schedules on real entries for the library catalogue instead of having to practice on unrelated examples in a text book.

Every few weeks large numbers of new entries, each on its own slip of paper, had to be inserted into the catalogue. Incidentally, that is why most libraries avoid printing their full catalogue in book form: because new items are constantly being added to stock and worn-out items removed, the physical form of the catalogue has to be flexible enough to permit these constant changes, and paper slips or cards are therefore used so that notification of a change will not ruin the careful order of the catalogue.

I used to detest this work. There are special rules for arranging strings of words into one alphabetical sequence. It is not as simple as it may seem. Words like 'a' and 'the' are ignored, so are their counterparts in foreign languages, and that meant being able to recognise them even though I had taken only French and German at school. Then each letter of every other word in the heading and in the title had to be taken into consideration before the entry could finally be placed in sequence. Great care and attention are vital, but my attention used to relax after the first half-hour or so and, as we had to leave our efforts jutting out of the place we had selected, it was galling to have mistakes pointed out by senior staff who checked them all and left the evidence of our carelessness sticking up like porcupine quills for all to see.

Such attention to accuracy is not old-maidish fussiness. A misplaced entry is as bad as not having the entry in at all, for if the reader looks where he should look he will not spot the wrongly sited item and will assume, therefore, that the library does not possess that particular work. However, hurt pride is a wonderful stimulus to achieve accuracy.

There were other tasks, of course. Books requiring attention at the binders and completed volumes of periodicals all had to be listed before despatch and checked on return. But it was the unforeseen readers' queries that I enjoyed most. Some were too difficult for the junior staff to handle, and these we quickly passed on to more experienced hands, watching to see where we should have looked so that next time we would know a little more.

Then one day there was a job we never expected to have to do. The German air force turned its attention from London and Coventry and made a number of attacks on the North-West, first Liverpool and then, just before Christmas 1940, it was Manchester's turn. At my home in the suburbs we huddled for most of the night in our air-raid shelter, and when we looked out, during lulls in the bombing, it was obvious from the red glow and smoke in the sky that the centre of the city had been badly hit.

Next morning, as I picked my way past gutted buildings, through tangles of hose pipes and debris (for the public transport could not run for some time), I hardly dared think of what I might find when eventually I reached the library. Finally I was there and turned the last corner. The four-storey furniture shop on one side of our building was burned out and still smoking. The bank and office block on the other was razed practically to the ground.

But Rylands, separated from both, fortunately, by a narrow street on either side, was safe. In fact, one of the stick of incendiary bombs that had destroyed the other buildings had fallen on our roof which was nearly flat and covered with a very thick layer of asphalt, and it had not managed to burn its way through to set the building on fire. We had been saved by Victorian lavishness, for the roof did not really need to be that thick for normal purposes.

Nevertheless, it was obvious that next time we might not be so lucky. Wooden packing cases were hurriedly obtained, all normal work stopped, and everyone helped wrap up the treasures of the library in waterproof paper and cram them into the boxes. The intention was to take them into the country for safe-keeping until after the war. But the weight of a large quantity of books had been overlooked, especially since these, being very old, were made up of rag paper (the thickest and heaviest of all papers) or vellum or parchment leaves, and bound in heavy leather, metal or ivory bindings.

When the first full packing case was lifted for loading on to a trolley, the bottom fell out—it was only nailed on, and we had to repack all the others, reducing the quantity of books in each. Afterwards we wanted to laugh, but at the time it was all too urgent and serious. Needless to say, after these most precious of our items had been evacuated no more bombs fell anywhere near the library.

Shortly after this, in February 1943, having reached the age of eighteen, I was called up for military service, and as a field gunner in the Royal Regiment of Artillery I was soon far away from books and libraries.

3

JUNIOR IN A CITY PUBLIC LIBRARY

THERE FOLLOWED FOUR YEARS of uncertainty, most of it spent in the Middle East. Unexpectedly, during a short period of leave, I found myself visiting Egyptian tombs and pyramids that reminded me of the papyrus documents back home. Then my regiment moved north into Syria. Damascus itself was only just down the road and I thought of the famous old illuminated manuscript in which the monastic artist used a large decorated capital P to depict the story of St Paul's escape from Damascus. In the bowl of the letter we see a view of the city. From the top of the stem his friends are lowering a rope. It dangles right down the stem of the letter, six or seven inches along the margin of the page, painted to resemble the city wall, and at the end of the rope is St Paul in a basket. To stand outside those very walls made the past again seem much more real to me.

Eventually it was all over. My turn came to be demobilised and I was a civilian again. What next? Many ex-servicemen had no desire to return to their old occupations, but I still could not think of anything else I would rather do. However, I decided not to go back to Rylands though Dr. Guppy, the librarian, and the Board of Governors were agreeable to my returning if I so wished.

In academic libraries such as Rylands and those of the universities there are no real career prospects for non-graduates. They are wonderful training grounds for anyone, and today some of the more progressive university librarians have created limited career prospects for non-graduate but professionally qualified librarians within the middle ranges of their salary scales which are particularly attractive to some girl Chartered Librarians; but the top senior university library posts are, reasonably enough, not open to non-graduates however well-qualified they may be otherwise.

I could have obtained an ex-serviceman's grant from the Government in order to take a university degree. (Now-a-days, one would apply to one's local education authority after being offered a university place.) Instead I applied for a junior post in the Manchester Public Library service; but now I think it would have been more sensible to have taken a degree first. At the time I thought it extremely unlikely that I should get a second grant to study for my professional qualifications after graduating (official attitudes have since changed) so, as I had just become engaged to be married, I concentrated upon the shortest possible course.

I must admit that it was with some trepidation that I made the switch from the academic to the public library world: there were bound to be differences and I should only know the extent of these and how they would affect me by experiencing them, but I was encouraged in my decision by the high regard in which the Manchester public library system was held.

After being interviewed by the City Librarian I was offered the post and told to report the following Monday morning to one of the larger branches out in the suburbs. Gradually I became accustomed to the different method of issuing books and to a totally unfamiliar kind of book stock. There were modern novels and light non-fiction as well as some of the more advanced material. The branch library has to present a selection rather than attempt to offer a comprehensive coverage of subjects. The daily inrush of children to the separate junior department as soon as the schools had finished for the day was also new and something of an ordeal at first.

Above all, I found the different tempo of work strange after four years of army life. A busy branch library on a Saturday afternoon with a number of us on the counter all checking in loans and issuing new ones as fast as we could was a totally new experience. In any one week public library staffs do not work more than thirty-eight hours, but some of these will be (by rota) on one or two evenings—probably up to eight or nine o'clock— and on a Saturday, when one's friends are free. University libraries also operate such systems and are likely to stay open until ten o'clock on weekday evenings.

One of the advantages is that one can go shopping for new clothes, or go out for the day on one's afternoon or day off during the week, and thus miss the frenzy of trying to make a choice at the height of the Saturday afternoon rush and having to travel when roads and public transport are full of everyone else wanting to do the same thing. Certainly it is a way of life that has to be accepted with its drawbacks as well as its advantages if one chooses this career.

One of the fascinations of a public library is the wide assortment of people that one meets. In an academic library the range is much narrower, but in the rate-supported service one sees them all from don to tramp. Teachers and students working to tight educational timetables can be expected to want to borrow texts related to their course of study, but the same people are equally likely to ask for a do-it-yourself manual for car or household maintenance, a travel book to help plan next year's holiday, or a thriller to relax with. A housewife may want a pleasant romance to read during a quiet half-hour, a standard work on the psychology of the infant and something else on political science for the university extra-mural classes she attends on Wednesday evenings when her husband stays home as babysitter.

Then there is always the voracious reader who arrives each week with a list of new books of all types which were recommended in the magazine sections of the previous Sunday's papers. 'These got a very good review. Have you got them in

stock and if not can I reserve them?' The better your stock and
the more sympathetic and efficient your service, the more varied
will be the requests for information and reading matter of all
kinds. For nothing succeeds faster than success. Very soon one
gets to know what will particularly interest many of the regular
readers, and the common bond will widen one's circle of
acquaintances and friends.

Yet every efficient organisation generates its own routine of
monotonous yet important chores that need to be done well if the
service is to function properly, and every trainee librarian must
be prepared to accept a fair share of these unless the service point
is so large and busy that special clerical staff can be employed to
run that side of things. Borrowed books are eventually returned.
They have to be replaced in correct sequence on the shelves.
Borrowers, when browsing to decide what they shall read, do
not always replace books in their correct place. So, if the library
is not to look like a badly-run secondhand bookshop, someone
has to rearrange and tidy the stock at least once a day. Usually
that is done in the morning when things are quiet.

Not all borrowers remember to return their books punctually
in spite of having to pay a small fine if their loans do become
overdue. Postal reminders have to be addressed to the forgetful.
Reserved books have to be located in the issue and clearly marked
so that, when they are returned, they are kept off the public
shelves until the borrower has had a chance to call in and collect
them.

Simple repairs to torn pages will be carried out on the spot, but
books in need of more serious attention will have to be listed and
packed up for despatch to a bindery. None of this is really exciting
work but the junior staff have to take their share of it as well as
doing more professional duties because it is uneconomical to expect the senior professional staff, who receive higher salaries, to
waste time which they could otherwise spend more profitably in
exercising their special skills for the benefit of the public.

Shortly after my appointment it happened that a special department was created in the central reference library to cater for the scientist and technologist. In the late 1940's several of the larger public reference libraries were departmentalising their stocks so that specialist staff could be trained to offer a more intensive service. My academic reference training at Rylands was presumably considered likely to make me a useful assistant in the new section and I was transferred to the staff of the Technical Library in the central building.

Once more here was new material with which to become familiar, and a new type of reader to meet and get to know. In addition to the students and teachers who had made up our largest class of reader at Rylands there were now businessmen, engineers and scientists, often posing their enquiries personally or by telephone in technical jargon. They would ask about quick methods of de-rusting iron, the viscosity of a liquid, or Laplace transforms for electrical calculations. Someone with the makings of a new invention would wish to search through our thousands upon thousands of patents, both British and foreign, before continuing with further development work, in order to check whether anyone else had registered the same or a similar idea.

As far as the routine side of the work was concerned there were no overdue notices to be sent out, for this was a department for reference use only within the library itself. Instead, there were many issues of technical journals to be received and checked in each week to ensure that no issue was missed. Particularly for the technologist and scientist the periodical is a very important means of keeping abreast of new developments all over the world, and every new issue must be at least scanned just as the man in the street glances over his daily paper for fear of missing something interesting. Textbooks, monographs and treatises are the repositories of basic principles and accounts of all that has been discovered to date, but the periodical concerns itself with new science in the making all over the world.

Unfortunately for the intending reader, knowledge is being advanced so rapidly that more and more new titles are being added to the already over-long list of such journals. People begin to ask how they can possibly check through them all and do their day's work as well. The librarian begins to wonder where he is going to store all the extra paper that records this information explosion. As a part solution, at least, towards making sure that one can be aware without delay of what has been written recently about one's subject, there are yet other periodicals which serve to index the information in all the others!

Supply firms also use technical journals for advertising new products and services, for the smart industrialist wants to know what is new in equipment just as the smart woman reads advertisements in *Vogue* or *The Queen* to learn where she may buy the latest fashions in clothes. A go-ahead firm cannot afford not to know what is new.

Technical journals are particularly expensive, and a large reference department will have hundreds of these on its list of holdings. Many are in the English language, but others are in the language of their country of origin: Germany, France, Russia, Japan, China and so on. Special libraries like these are the only places where one can be practically certain of finding the article one saw last month—or last year—or about five years ago, when the only certain knowledge is that the issue is not at home or in the office.

Such libraries carefully file away each issue of the most important journals in their particular field, perhaps even having them bound into permanent book form as each volume is completed, and this all entails painstaking care behind the scenes. The more senior staff will also be doing their share of duty in the back rooms: selecting new items for stock, preparing bibliographies or planning special displays but more of that later. I had other things to learn before I could share in that. Most of

my time, as at Rylands, was spent in attending to readers' requests
for books and helping them as far as I was able before handing
over to staff with greater experience.

For the outsider perhaps the most unexpected request to hear
of in a technical library is one for information about cocktails.
However, brewing, wine-making and similar arts are basically
technical matters, and the librarian classifies books on the subject
as one of the many manufacturing processes. Thus, one day, we
were confronted by an immaculate barman, resplendent in the
uniform of the large hotel across the road. He wanted ideas for
new cocktails. Had we any recipes? Of course we had, and the
books were fetched.

About twenty minutes later they were returned by the now
beaming cocktail shaker, who frequently came back after that
for odd moments of obviously profitable research. That he
firmly believed in the rewarding of good service (like most
hotel staff) was abundantly clear, for, after his first success, he
never failed to show his appreciation of our efforts by proffering
a tip which we were not allowed to accept.

In those days one had to pass a preliminary examination set
by the Library Association before one could begin to prepare
for the advanced examinations leading to qualification as
Associate and then Fellow of the Library Association. This I
sat shortly after I was demobilised, and when I learned that I had
passed, I decided to go to one of the new library schools.

Before the war there had been only one, a post-graduate
school at London University. Now, because the profession was
awakening to the fact that part-time training (the old-fashioned
way) was not only very slow but also not the best way of going
about things because many more qualified people were needed
quickly, the government encouraged the setting up of several
new schools. The one at Manchester was in its second year.

My application was accepted, and I enrolled as a student in the
autumn term of 1947, along with about twenty other ex-

servicemen and women. We attended lectures on library law and administration, library planning, cataloguing and classification, assistance to readers, book selection, the history of printing and the techniques of book production, and English literature. The syllabus has since been changed, so further detail is now pointless, but we also visited libraries of all kinds in order to compare methods and standards of provision so that we might cram much experience, even if at second hand, into a short time. We also did much reading and argued incessantly among ourselves about what we were seeing and hearing.

For us all it was a fascinating experience. We knew we were being treated as guinea pigs to some extent. These schools were new. Our lecturers were, for the most part, equally new to the teaching profession, though they had pre-war library qualifications and experience. Yet we were all aware of the new impetus which was affecting the profession and we were determined to make the most of our opportunities, not just for our own sakes but also to create new and better standards of library provision. We all were very conscious of the four or more war years we had each had to waste in the forces.

We worked through that bitterly cold winter of fuel shortages and power cuts. Our accommodation, not wanted by any other section of the college, was not all that comfortable. It was a large ex-laboratory, tremendously high and hard to heat, but it had its amusing features also. For some inexplicable reason several sacks of dried peas had been dumped in one corner. The room was so large that they were never in our way, but they tended to irritate us somewhat nevertheless. That was, until we found a use for them. Somebody discovered a knot-hole in the old wooden floor through which we could see into the room beneath. From then on, when we were at a loose end between lectures, we would send odd showers of peas cascading down to startle the folk below. We dared not do it too frequently, of course, for that might have encouraged someone to investigate.

Then it was spring, then summer and examination time. When it was all over, bar waiting anxiously for the results, we went our various ways, back to our libraries, for we had been granted leave of absence by our employing authorities for the duration of the course.

Twenty years later it is interesting to take another look at some of those ex-student friends of mine. Several are in charge of municipal library services up and down the country. One is the Librarian of a large northern county. Between times he was a County Branch Librarian and then a City Librarian. A few of us eventually went into the expanding world of college libraries, spending some time on the way in getting different experience in public and county branches and then in special technical libraries such as those maintained by I.C.I. Ltd., and guided missile divisions of the aircraft industry.

At least one of the girls ended up working in an American library before she got married and left the profession. Another went to Western Australia to help create a new public library service there—and then married her boss, the State Librarian. A third, whom I remember particularly vividly for her great vitality and sense of fun, worked for a while as a mobile librarian, taking a county library service out to country farms and hamlets in a specially equipped van (a very interesting and rewarding aspect of service). Then she married an engineer whom she had met at a Union dance when he, too, was a student. There was also Beryl. I never did discover what became of her. All I can remember is a picture in the local newspaper showing her chained to a lamp post and being rescued by cowboys during the rag week procession that year.

The then Head of the School is also in the United States now: the Associate Dean of the Graduate School of Library and Information Science at the University of Pittsburgh. His fellow lecturer is the present Head of the Manchester School, and the third member of the original team in 1947 has returned to Wales to spend an active retirement not wholly unconnected with her former profession, for she is a member of the newly formed Library Advisory Council for Wales.

4

THE QUALIFIED LIBRARIAN

IN ALL BRANCHES of the public service, at local municipal and at national civil service levels, there are clearly defined quotas for the number of staff in each unit, and the appropriate salary within nationally regulated scales of pay is fixed by local or ministerial decision for each post. A similar but less rigid method of deciding the establishment of staff also applies to many large and industrial undertakings. That is, salaries are fixed according to the duties connected with a given post rather than by the ability of any one individual; and, at least for the public services, the rule is inflexible.

No matter how efficient they may be, no one in this kind of organisation can be promoted to a higher-paid post unless there is a vacancy within the establishment for that particular grade. Non-public undertakings, on the other hand, are less affected by such attitudes and may well increase a person's salary as a reward for good service, though still employing him on the same type of work, rather than run the risk of losing him and his experience to a competitor.

When I returned to work at the end of my course, therefore, it was to await not only the result of my examinations but also a suitable vacancy in a higher graded post that was considered to be within the range of my ability. For this waiting period I was placed on the staff of the Commercial Department of the Reference Library, still in a junior capacity, and I was highly delighted, for if my work in the Technical Department prior to my departure for library school had not been considered promising I would have found myself being moved into a less demanding position.

As it was, I realised that I was being given further opportunity to widen my experience, that I was fairly high on the list for junior promotion; and that, when it did come, such promotion would be interesting. In other words, I would receive true advancement into a busy or exacting section rather than into a dull backwater which required some degree of seniority as a palliative for boredom as much as for any other reason.

The Commercial Department was on the ground floor of the Central Reference Library, deliberately sited close to the main entrance. The stock comprised a mixture of five different types of material, each tending to supplement the usefulness of the others. There was a basic collection of standard textbooks and monographs on all aspects of business: economics, law, management, buying and selling, advertising, banking, accountancy and similar topics. Not just one or two books on each, as one tends to find in a branch library where the stock has to show variety through the whole range of knowledge in spite of limited shelving space, but a wide selection of similar titles by different authors to give readers the opportunity of comparing the views of a number of experts on each subject.

People from the city offices were the main users of these. By day some of the callers were likely to be senior members of firms checking a point of company law or familiarising themselves with new management techniques. In the evenings junior members of office staffs would arrive after a quick snack in one of the local cafés and settle down with their correspondence course notes and our books on accountancy or banking until closing time came at nine o'clock.

In a separate sequence there were the directories, often the source of some of our most spectacular triumphs in information work. Those who live in medium or large-sized towns are probably quite accustomed to the fact that there is a *Kelly's*

Directory for their town, and that such works can be used to discover who lives at a certain number in a particular street, or the makers of this or that type of commodity. Similarly, telephone directories may also be used to ascertain the address of a person or firm, as well as their telephone number. However, there is a tendency to consider such research as a local, rather than a national, let alone an international, matter.

It can be rather startling, therefore, to find a comprehensive collection of directories in a well-stocked library, with a volume for practically every town in the British Isles, plus special directories of manufacturers. Some of the latter attempt to list all kinds of firm: others concentrate on the products relating to a clearly defined range of goods, for the electrical industry, perhaps, or even just for the radio section of it. That, however, is not the end of such a collection, for there are similar publications, general and specialised, for other countries (naturally so, when one thinks for a moment).

Under the directory stands we had an enormous collection of huge volumes lying flat, one or two to each shelf. This was our map collection. There were the British Ordnance Survey series of $1''$, $2\frac{1}{2}''$ and $6''$ sheets; the Geological Survey and the Land Utilisation maps; together with world atlases, foreign as well as British.

The fourth broad category of material consisted of periodicals (magazines and newspapers to the man in the street). We tried to display all the important titles, plus some of the lesser publications, relating to our special field of commerce. The term has varying connotations, though. To some people, as far as periodicals were concerned, it meant the *Kinematograph Weekly*, for details of new releases and booking arrangements. To others it might mean *The Ambassador* or the *Drapers' Record*. The printer might ask for *Point of Sale*. We were always intrigued by those who carefully scanned through the *Investors' Guardian* and the *Investors' Chronicle*, for here were financial wizards in action.

There was even the human interest story attached to some of these papers. A daily stream of regular visitors called simply to check on the whereabouts of a husband or boyfriend, though they were not private inquiry agents as you may have imagined. Manchester is a port, albeit an inland one, but it tends to be forgotten, or not even realised, that some of its citizens are regularly working thousands of miles away as the crews of cargo ships all over the world.

Although it would be known that a certain ship was sailing for a particular port, say in South America, its movements after arrival there, and its eventual return to Manchester, might well depend upon the vagaries of trade and the destination of any cargo found waiting at ports en route. Airmail letters from the crew would not take long to reach Britain, but this was not the quickest way of learning whether a ship would be docking today or next month.

The sources of this information, and indeed for similar news of other ports all over the world are two daily newspapers never seen on the average newsagent's counter. They are *Lloyd's List* and the *Journal of Commerce*, and they receive their news of shipping movements by radio, so it is possible to follow a given ship day by day as it moves in and out of port. Naturally, shipping agents use this service even more than do the relatives of those on board the vessels.

The fifth bastion of the Commercial Library's information service was our clippings file, and its compilation involved continuous activity during our quieter moments. To have seen us at work on this must have been a deceptive experience. We would sit apparently reading a newspaper or magazine. Was this what librarians were paid for, then? What was not so obvious was the fact that the newspaper would be a day or two old, and that, every now and then, we would cut out a paragraph or two. We were searching discarded periodicals, mainly the leading national and financial dailies, for interesting items, not only of a commercial nature but also relating to passing events of particular interest.

Each clipping had to be marked with the title and date of the newspaper from which it had been taken. Then it was mounted on a standard-size sheet, given a heading and its subject entered in a card index. The sheets were then filed in a bank of cabinets. This was our memory store.

A member of the government might be touring the area, with an itinerary spread over several days. An enquirer might wish to know, nearer the time, the exact programme of visits on one of the days, probably adding that he wished he had cut the published programme out of last week's paper. Well, we had, and the clipping could be produced within a minute. Export and import controls can be altered as the need arises, and the revised regulations are issued through Her Majesty's Stationery Office. They are also likely to be reported in the financial columns, and again, our clippings file often came in very useful.

At other times our work made us look more like detectives than librarians. Our ability to answer difficult enquiries only served to encourage people to bring along even more complex problems, and we were delighted with such challenges to the library's stock and our own special skills, though at times even our hopes were daunted by the size of the problem.

One of those legendary successes, in which (to be honest) luck always played some part, was the story of the lady and the prayer book. A story that was told, sooner or later, to every new member of the staff so as to inculcate the belief that in a good library practically no information problem is completely devoid of solution.

This person, as far as we know, had never been in the central library before, but she had a problem, and somehow she had heard that the Commercial Library and Information Service was a good place to try first. She wished to buy an expensively bound prayer book as a present for a school girl in Australia, the daughter of a distant relative who had gone out as a young girl herself and later married an Australian. Apparently letters between the families had been very sporadic, and it suddenly occurred to our enquirer that she really knew so little about the Australian family that she could not be certain of the schoolgirl's religion. Obviously, if the prayer book turned out to be of a denomination other than that of the recipient the present would be an awful blunder. Yet how could the library staff possibly find the answer?

Here luck came into the picture. The people in Australia happened to live in one of the very large cities, so that meant that there was a directory of its inhabitants, and we had a copy of it. As in most of the large English directories there were lists of organisations, municipal offices, public services and schools, which were sub-divided to show whether they were run by the state, or private owners, or churches, which were again sub-divided according to denomination.

Had the name of the girl's school ever been mentioned in a letter? This meant going home to check through carefully hoarded links with the other side of the world. A day of two later the lady returned with the name of a school. It was checked against the various lists and shown to be under the care of the Church of England. Luck on its own would not have been enough if the librarians who dealt with that enquiry had not been very well-trained and rich in experience of such work.

On another occasion we searched and searched without any success. A businessman told us that he needed to know the length of the cotton staple used before the war by the mills of one of the middle European countries. From this he could tell whether they concentrated on producing good or poor quality cloths. His recollection was that the latter had been the case, but he needed to verify this, and it was not only important but urgently so.

In the end we realised that outside help was needed, so we

telephoned the laboratories of a famous textile research institute. Such organisations frequently refuse to deal with enquiries from non-members (after all, to supply information costs money) but usually they cheerfully co-operate with reference librarians, simply because they may well need to use the reference library themselves, on occasion.

The institute staff could not find anything relevant in their records, either, but they thought that another member of their team might well know the answer. Unfortunately, he was away on the day we telephoned, though he would be back in the laboratory next day. That did not seem too long to wait for such an awkward piece of information, but it transpired that our enquirer was catching an early train to London before we could possibly telephone the institute. Then he had a brainwave. If we telephoned the institute as soon as we arrived on duty next morning he would dash out of the train at Crewe, where there was a delay of about twenty minutes later in the morning and ring us for the information.

On the following day everything went according to plan. The research worker was back in his laboratory and, as forecast, he did know the answer to our question. The businessman telephoned from Crewe, and was able to use the information at his conference in London.

It is possible to offer only a sample of life in a busy city commercial reference library, but picture a constant procession of people with questions to be answered, either by their own efforts or with our aid. At times the telephone never seemed to stop ringing, either, but it was stimulating and very satisfying work, probably because, more often than not, we could see the product of our efforts in the form of a specific piece of information.

In this kind of librarianship there seems to be less of the fetching of books for others to use and more of the librarian making information sources work for others. This attraction it shares with special librarianship, where the library is the centre of an information service for a particular firm or group of companies.

Much of this work is naturally the product of team effort. Sometimes one works alone on an enquiry, but the good librarian is always the one who never hesitates to admit when he has exhausted all the avenues of exploration that he can think of and then gets the advice of his colleagues. The success of the library service is our aim, and we are not interested in glorifying the work of any one individual.

This lesson I was fortunate to learn very early in my career, in that very department I have just described. At my first meeting with Mr. Jones, the Librarian-in-Charge, he told me never to hesitate to ask for assistance. 'It is no disgrace to admit temporary defeat', he said. 'Some days we are brighter than others, so, on occasions, you will find me asking you for ideas, even though I have much more experience'.

That was a very kind way of putting things, for any new member of a staff always feels a little out of things and useless at first, yet is naturally hesitant to draw attention to any inadequacy, even if it is due to a reasonable lack of experience in that particular section. Such hesitancy can be very dangerous to the work of the team, because an enquirer could be sent away without the information he requires.

With so much to occupy my mind it did not seem very long before the examination results were published and I learned that I had been successful in all papers, thus qualifying for registration as a Chartered Librarian, an Associate of the Library Association. The first hurdle had been surmounted, and I was a full member of my professional association. Nevertheless, I decided not to stop studying, for there was still a Fellowship of the Library Association to aim at. In those days one gained this final distinction by further examination. Today the award is reached through the submission of a thesis.

I stayed in the Commercial Department for almost a year. Then, in May 1949, I was moved on. I was informed that I had been promoted to Senior Assistant, and that my new duties would take me back to the Branch where I had started. Now, however, I would be, in effect, deputy to the Branch Librarian. I had already seen branch library service through the eyes of a junior. Now I was to take some part in training and guiding such assistants, as well as taking a more professional share of the day to day activity.

5

LIFE IN THE BRANCHES

THE CHORLTON BRANCH was then the second largest of some thirty in the city, an oldish building, designed on lines very similar to many others of the early period of library development about the second half of last century. In fact it had been the fifth branch to be set up in Manchester, just sixteen years after the passing of the first Public Libraries Act.

Its stock in 1949 amounted to some 25,000 volumes, and there were about 30,000 people in the residential area surrounding it. I was the only man on a staff of six girls and a woman librarian. Not since junior school days had I had to take orders from a woman, but the prospect did not engender any embarrassment. I had already grown accustomed to the fact that the men in the profession were greatly out-numbered, and all that I have ever asked of those superior to me, male or female, is that they should be efficient, fair and full of common sense.

Any manager with these attributes is more than likely to win the respect and confidence of those under him, and librarianship certainly offers equal professional opportunities and promotion possibilities to men and women so long as they have the right qualifications. The Head of the National Reference Library for Science and Technology is a woman; the Head of the National Lending Library for Science and Technology is a man.

But to return to Chorlton: it was necessary to present myself in a way soundly professional yet sympathetically human to the girls under me if I were to develop into a good and useful Senior

Assistant. I had to be prepared to live with mutual admiration sessions in the staff room when someone arrived in the latest fashion in shoes or a new dress. On the other hand, the girls had to tolerate a certain mount of teasing from me, and we all quickly settled down without much awkwardness. Personnel management affects all aspects of daily work, and all such management requires the ability to serve those below as well as those above one if an organisation of any kind is to work happily and efficiently.

So much for our side of the library counter. However, the best and most hard-working of local government officials often get themselves a bad name, because they are so busy being efficient among themselves that they forget to be human to the ratepayers they are supposed to be serving. I had to be doubly conscious of this pitfall now, not only as far as my own conduct went, but also because I had to assist the Branch Librarian to train the junior staff to have the same outlook. *Do unto others as you would be done by* is perhaps no bad motto for anybody, and particularly an official, to adopt.

The readership of a branch varies according to the social make-up of the locality. It is dangerous to generalise, but levels of intelligence and of interest in reading often vary from suburb to suburb within an urban area, so that a branch might be in a district where the people have very wide interests, borrowing heavily, and with equal avidity, current fiction of importance and non-fiction works on social or political problems, drama, music, history and so on.

On the other hand, it might be in an area where the general interest in reading of any sort is slight, or where the emphasis is on very light reading. The ratio of library to non-library user in such a district will be smaller than in the first example, and the intensity of demand might well be less as well. The librarian has to be aware of the range and types of interest in his area and to vary his stock to suit the local need.

Chorlton happened to be in a very keen reading area. Television, then still a new toy as it developed rapidly after the wartime standstill, was making some inroads into people's reading time, just as it does now, but it had not stopped the keen reader altogether, as had been forecast. Indeed, certain of the more cultural programmes were widening the reading tastes of viewers.

A large proportion of our members were very much aware of the vast range of works that a good library service can supply. Such people took it for granted that we would be as familiar with the publishing of new titles within their sphere of interest as they were (after all, this was our profession), that a reasonable proportion of such books would be quickly available on our shelves, and that the rest could be obtained for them without undue delay.

The Librarian and I both took a natural personal interest in reading the advance notices of publication issued through the book trade. There were also the general reviewing periodicals such as *The Times Literary Supplement*, and the special book sections in the leading Sunday and weekend newspapers like *The Observer*, *New Statesman*, and *Spectator*. Some of these we found time to study at work; the rest had to be covered at home. No one actually said that we had to do this homework. We did it because we were naturally interested and wanted to.

Every library has certain peak periods of activity, according to the business and social habits of those who use it. By and large, evenings and Saturdays are often the busiest time for a branch lending library service. That is when the majority of people who go out to work have the time to spare for their own interests. Housewives, school children, and retired people will tend to visit their library at certain times during the day.

Thus the various parts of each day affect the work load of the whole staff, and the librarian plans ahead so that maximum numbers of staff are on duty at peak service times, and yet no one works more than the nationally agreed local government working week expressed in hours. (Thirty-eight to be precise). The Librarian and I took alternate shifts, so that, although we both might be on duty for part of a day, one of us, at least, was there from first thing in a morning until closing time at night.

The bulk of the staff spent the first hour of each morning in tidying and rearranging the books on the shelves. The notice board outside might well proclaim, as ours did, that the library did not open until 10 a.m., but nevertheless, the staff on early duty had to be there by 9 a.m., so that some of the basic clearing up could be completed before the public were admitted. Readers can never be guaranteed to keep the books in order, and if the classification scheme is to mean anything, then the staff must ensure that the collections remain in sequence so that any title may be found easily and quickly.

The Librarian, or some other senior member of the staff such as myself, could utilise the same hour to check part of the stock, gradually working right round the library. This physical checking is done for several important reasons. Damaged books are generally noticed on return by the counter staff, and pulled out of circulation for repair, but there remain those books which gradually become too soiled with use to be issued again and those at the other end of the scale in which interest wanes.

A decision has to be taken with regard to the soiled books: are they to be replaced with a new copy, or simply withdrawn? The stamping on the date label will reveal the other category: those books no longer borrowed. Are these to be discarded, or put into store? Are they standard works for which demand is likely always to be slight, or are their subjects of seasonal interest, like sports? These are the titles to store, either in the stock room, or back at headquarters. If the titles are out of date they need replacing by new works or editions; if the subject of the book is only of passing topical interest, then the book might well be discarded after checking with the central stock editor to ensure that it is not the last copy in the system or region.

The space so cleared by this sorting process makes room for the new stock constantly being despatched from the central library, while the readers never get the feeling that the branch is more of a storehouse or a museum than a living, working collection of books. Once a week the Branch Librarian visited the central library to help choose new books for our stock.

The other early morning chore was the counting of the previous day's issue. This is a rather tedious task, but without statistics of some kind it is difficult for a librarian to be sure whether more or less use is being made of his service than in previous years. Issue statistics make a form of balance sheet for us. If we can show that we are issuing more books from a particular branch or department we can make a better case for having a larger bookfund and more staff—even larger premises—to deal with the increased load.

Once the count was over, a start was made on preparing the reminders about overdue books. These pre-printed postcards and letters had to catch the early post to ensure delivery first thing next morning.

Thus the first hour passed quickly for everyone, the first of the early shoppers began to trickle in, and certain of the assistants would be detailed to start an hour or two's duty on the counter. Boredom, staleness, and then almost inevitable rudeness to the public can be prevented if staff are not kept on one particular task all day long. So those on counter duty up to lunch time could generally expect to be on different tasks, perhaps in the workroom, during the afternoon.

A large branch will have a separate room for children's books. There should also be a separate, specialist, Children's Librarian, who will be partly responsible to the Branch Librarian and partly to the Librarian-in-Charge of Work with Young People back at headquarters.

Unfortunately, when I was at Chorlton there was a great shortage of such specialists in the Manchester system, and we had to manage as best we could. That meant that we all had to try to familiarise ourselves with the children's stock, even if we were not drawn to that type of service. For, let me admit it, not every librarian is suited temperamentally to service in the children's section, and those who do not enjoy close proximity to lots of children are better kept well away on other work. The children are the adult readers of the future: they need proper and sympathetic training in the efficient and happy use of libraries, or else they may well be driven away for ever.

One of my responsibilities was the supervision of readers' requests. Reservations for popular titles tend to build up alarmingly if a book or its author hits the headlines, or if he is a TV personality, or simply a good writer with a permanently large following. Everybody then wishes to read his latest book as soon as it comes out so that they may discuss it with their friends. The problem here is to decide how many extra copies should be obtained, and the librarian needs to be kept informed of the local demand.

Requests for books not stocked by the branch have also to be dealt with speedily and efficiently. Perhaps the reader was not exactly sure of the title or some other vital piece of bibliographical detail; perhaps the reader was all too sure. That was what was wrong with our Arthur Waley request mentioned in the Introduction. The full citation, the corrected citation, has to be entered on the special request form, if possible before it is sent to headquarters, and that often means careful checking through bibliographies at the branch.

At headquarters the requests are supplied by calling upon the stock of other branches, by special purchase, or by a loan from another library system; and, although I did not know it then, I was to find myself in charge of that work after my spell at Chorlton. In the meantime there were other things to do.

As hinted at earlier, the Senior Assistant of a branch library was expected to assume local responsibility during the absence of the Librarian, and the prospect was not in the least alarming. However, I was quickly made to realise that I had not allowed for the unexpected—or perhaps it was simply that I was too much of an optimist in my inexperience.

Whatever the reason, I soon began to think that the Librarian must have a crystal ball that told her when to keep out of the way by having an afternoon off. (We were entitled to these in lieu of evening or Saturday duty). For as soon as she went off duty things began to happen, and every time it was clearly not due to any negligence on my part or that of the staff, but it was still uncanny.

For example, it was decided by the library committee of the city council that our building should be re-wired, and new, more powerful lights installed. Actually, fluorescent tubes were becoming more plentiful after the war. The electricians arrived and began tearing out the old wiring and replacing it with new, crawling into all sorts of odd places to do so.

Off went the Librarian when it was her half-day, and within a matter of minutes afterwards (or so it seemed) one of the workmen missed a nail with his hammer and hit a water tank high in the roof. I suppose it must have been almost as old as the building, and the assault with the hammer was too much for it. Water began to pour out, and I (minding my own business downstairs) was expected to do something about it. It was no use arguing that I, a librarian, was as untutored about plumbing as was the electrician. I was in charge.

Where was the stop tap? Where was a plumber? Was it the water tank that fed the central heating boiler? Because, if so, the boiler fire would have to be drawn, or the whole place would blow up. After that, the sooner I reported the matter by telephone to the central library, the sooner would the necessary replacement be authorised.

On another occasion someone was taken ill in the library when I was in charge. In any public building there is always the chance that this will happen, though in fact it is a very rare event.

However, the first occasion can be a little startling, especially if the victim is alone.

Until that moment I had never seen anyone suffer a fit. Such things happen very suddenly: often there is no warning. After the person had been made comfortable I had to decide what to do next. Well-meant advice was coming in from all sides: 'I think she ought to be taken home', people were saying, but was this the sensible thing to do? Was there anyone in the house to look after her? Was she well enough, even after a rest, to be taken there, even in a taxi? It might seem melodramatic, but I chose to call for an ambulance, so that she could have a hospital check-up. If plumbing had not been on the library school curriculum, neither had medicine.

Not all incidents are of a serious nature, fortunately. Funny things happen far more frequently. Once when I was helping other members of the staff with a spell of counter duty one of our borrowers put his returned book on the ledge in front of me. I noticed that some small pieces of paper were sticking out from the top of the pages, but thought no more of them at that moment because I was engaged in finding the reader's ticket in the issue. Pieces of paper used as bookmarks can always be pulled out afterwards, before the books are shelved. However, the person in front of me suddenly made a startled grab at the book before I could hand him his ticket.

'Sorry', he said, 'I forgot to take these out. I put them there when I was reading in bed'. With that he waved the papers under my nose and then stuffed them into his pocket. What strange things people get up to in bed, I thought to myself: never yet had I found it necessary to use seven or eight one-pound notes as a bookmark—in or out of bed!

Over the years the suburb that was Chorlton had spread and spread. Eventually a small sub-branch had had to be opened to cater, however inadequately, for those residents who now lived too far from the main branch yet not really much nearer to any other of our branches. It was intended to replace the temporary accommodation (a tiny room in a church hall) with more suitable, custom-built premises, but no one knew when that might be.

In the meantime this satellite was staffed on a part-time basis from the main branch. The size of the stock, about 5,000 volumes, was far too small really but better than nothing at all in the vicinity, especially for the older people. The accommodation was equally under-sized, and at busy times even the staff of one had a hard job to re-shelve returned books or help someone to find a suitable book. I do not think any of us really liked taking a turn of duty out there, except one of the girls who lived quite near, and so, for once, was soon back home after work.

I spent ten very interesting and enjoyable months at Chorlton. From the Librarian I learned much about the running of lending libraries, and from her and the public I learned a lot about the senior official's responsibilities when dealing with people. The theory of the library school lectures on organisation and management was given practical application for me at Chorlton.

Then it was decided by the City Librarian that it was time for me to move on once more. I was translated back to the central library building and given a section of my own. The salary grading was no higher than that of a Senior Assistant, but I was in charge, even if I was ultimately responsible to the Chief Assistant Librarian, who controlled all the book purchasing and despatching operations, and was himself responsible for all this to the City Librarian.

6

BACK ROOM BOYS (AND GIRLS)

MY NEW TITLE was Assistant-in-Charge, Union Shelf Register, which could be rolled off the tongue in a most grandiloquent manner, and it impressed people more by the mystery of its jargon than for any other reason.

Even so the post was quite a responsible one in its own small way. When the Branch Librarians received requests for books not in their own stock they sent them off to headquarters—as I have already described. From now on these same requests would be landing daily on my desk, and I and my small staff of three had to find those books from somewhere. We also had to despatch new books to the branches after they had been processed in the Accessions Department, and receive back any items for storage in the central reserve stock.

My briefing for the new task was a salutary one. The section I was to take over had been running satisfactorily for years, but the last person in charge had just retired, and it was made quite clear to me that, good though everything was, I had to make it better. I was to approach all the operations with a clear, fresh mind and increase productivity. What was not said, though clearly implicit, was that, in due course, my successor would be given exactly the same instructions, no matter how mightily I had laboured. In the world of business no one is indispensable.

Those of us on the administrative staff who worked behind the scenes in the central building were not in daily contact with the public. Accordingly, we worked office hours, because there was no advantage to the service in spreading our activities over a library day.

Each morning's post brought in a further quantity of requests from the branches and mobile libraries. If any of the details concerning the author and the title were incomplete, one of the girls would check through special lists supplied by the British and American book trade and add the missing information.

These bibliographies are published each week in Britain and each month in the United States, and from them and the large volumes into which they cumulate it is possible to ascertain what was published last week, or last year, or even many years ago, and—equally important—the firm responsible for publishing it. Books published in other countries can be found by checking the trade or national bibliography of that country.

Once we were sure that we had the correct author and title details each request could then be checked against the special union catalogue of all the stock in the branches and the Central Lending Library. Once it was known where the books were a list of those items not immediately available from the central lending department downstairs was circulated to all branches. Any items supplied by the former were prepared for despatch to the requesting library later in the day.

A copy of the circulation list was then posted to each of the branches so that they might report by telephone next morning on the availability of every title. But this was only the easiest part of the work.

Some works were not listed in the union catalogue. These had to be searched for in the catalogue of the Reference Library, which had a stock exceeding 400,000 items, for occasionally it was possible to lend a duplicate or easily replaceable title to a branch. Otherwise we were able to report that, although no copy of the book was available for loan, the person needing it could consult it in the Reference Library, which was open from 9 a.m. to 9 p.m. on six days of the week.

LIBRARIANSHIP 1 A story out-of-doors: part of the holiday mobile library service to children in Nottinghamshire
2 The technical department of Manchester Central Reference Library

ALL IN A DAY'S WORK

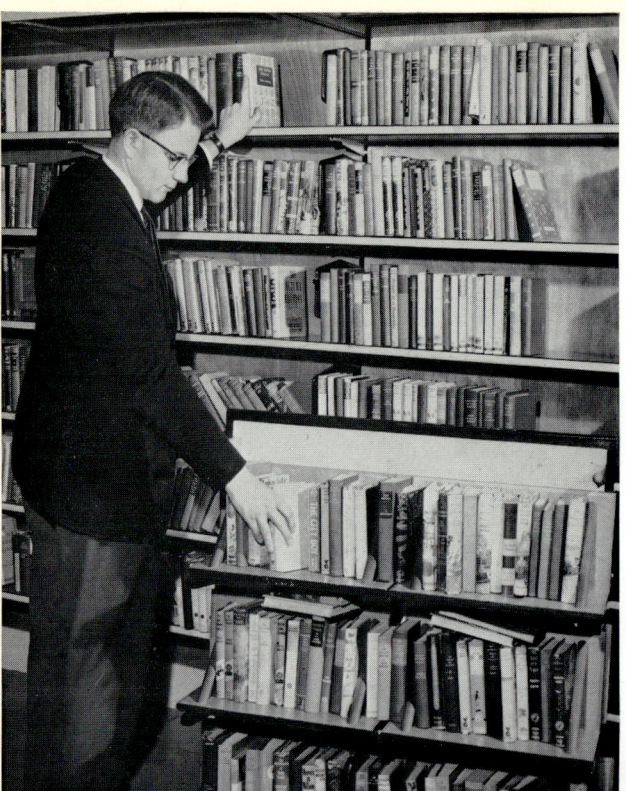

7 Returned books are sorted for reshelving

8 Cards are filed in the public catalogue

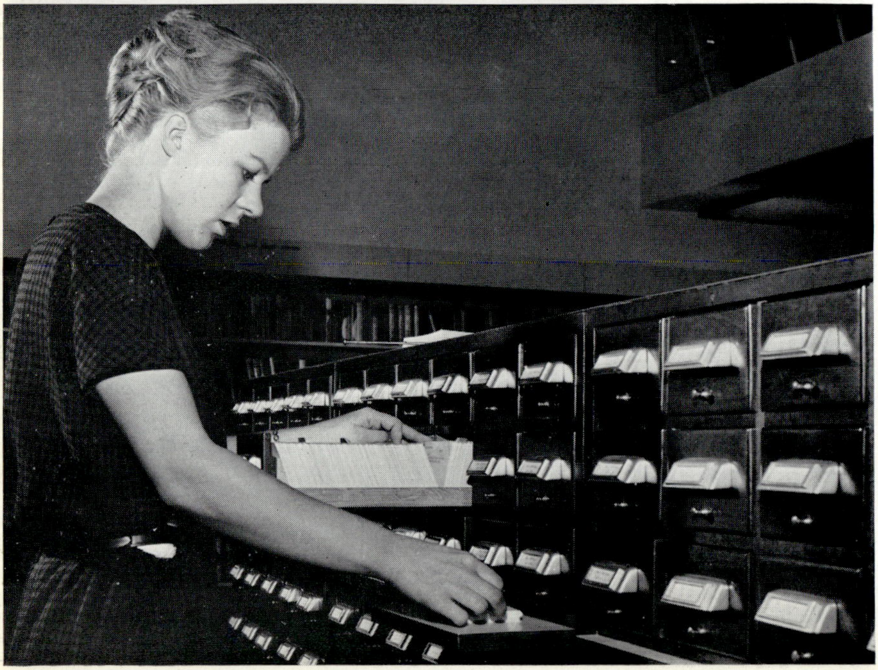

9 Advising a reader

ALL IN A DAY'S WORK

10 Using punched cards for issue records

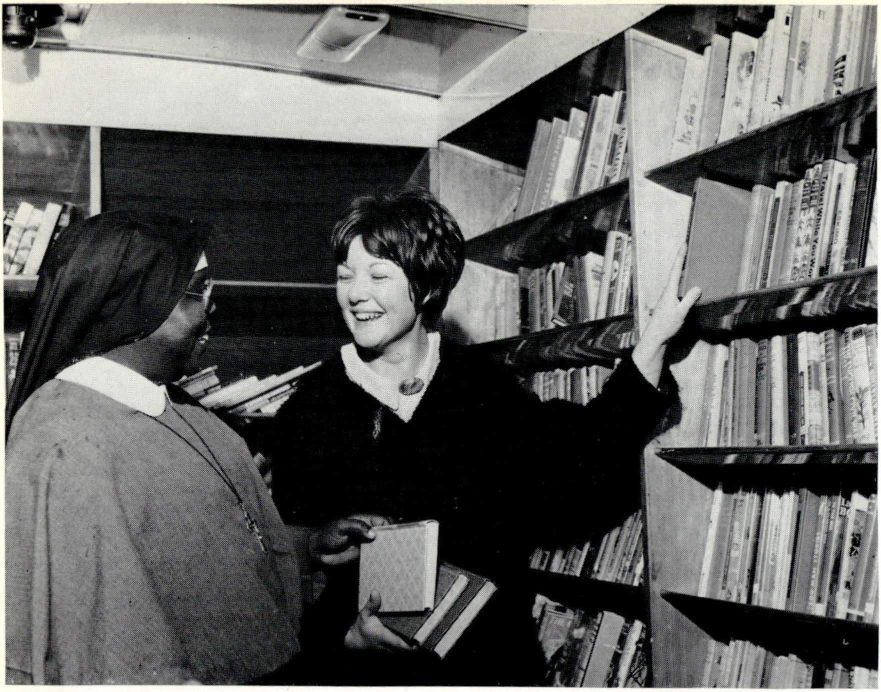

11 The mobile library service: a Schools Supervisor from Nigeria visits a van

LIBRARY SPECIALISATIONS

12 Research

13 AMCOS: sophisticated equipment for recording bibliographic information at Aldermaston

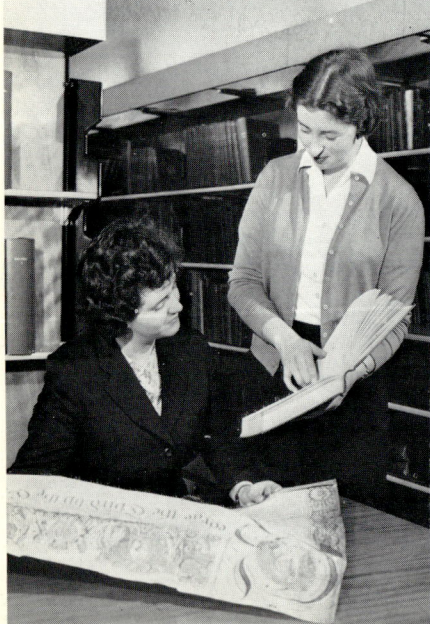

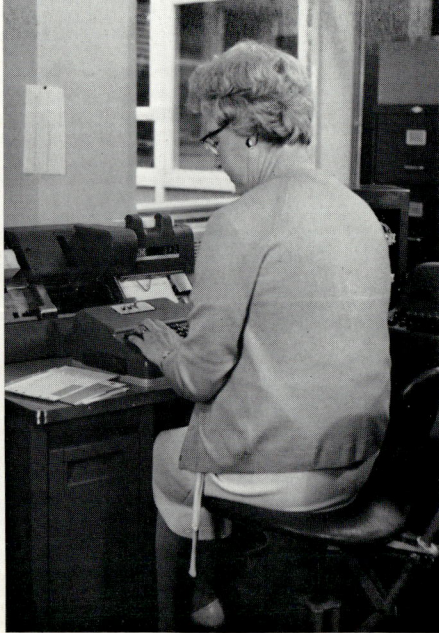

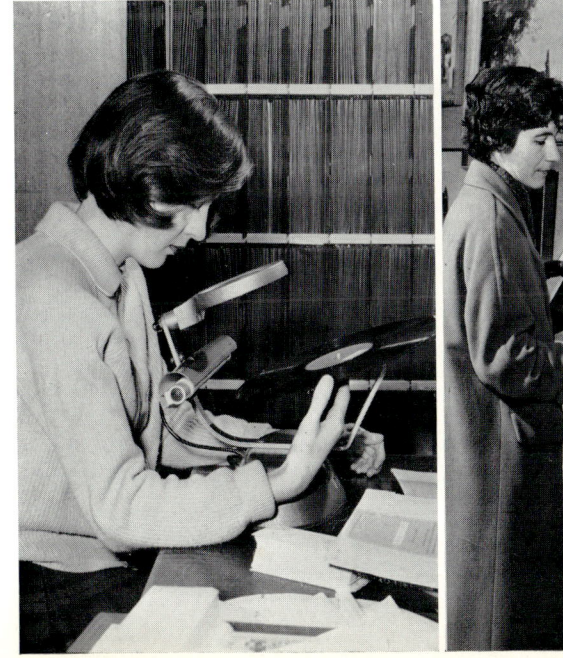

14 Junior library: Kingswood branch, Gloucestershire

LIBRARY SPECIALISATIONS

15 Record library: a disc is checked between issues

16 Selecting a picture for loan

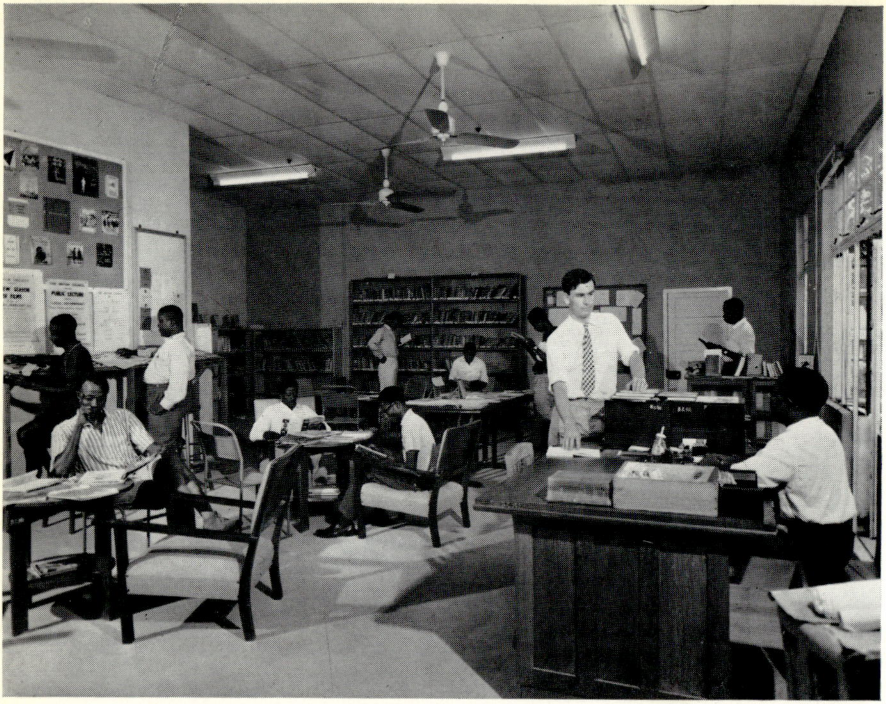

17 A new library is opened by the British Council in Sierra Leone

THE WIDER HORIZON: INTERNATIONAL EXCHANGES

18 Overseas librarians join their colleagues in Britain for a conference

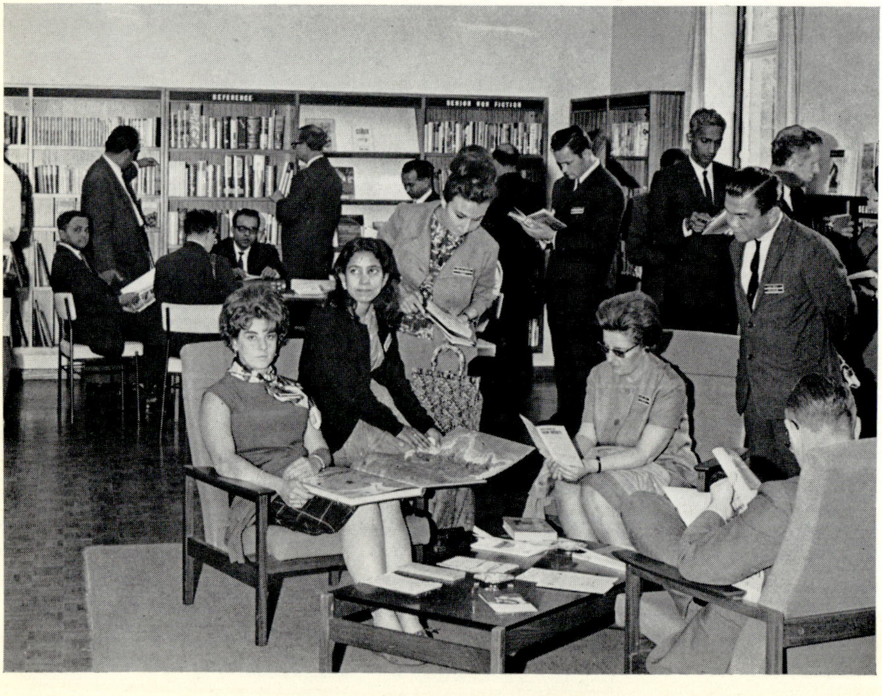

Subject requests needed a different technique. These were for any good books on this or that subject, for people who knew the sort of information they wanted but not the author or even the title of a relevant book. My task was to link one or more appropriate works to such requests, and then obtain them from somewhere in the system.

The prime need was for a good briefing on the request form, and for this I depended upon the staff who originally accepted the request and were unable to meet it from their own branch stock. I needed to know how much detail was required, whether the approach had to be historical or up-to-date, elementary or advanced, and all my hard-won experience in the techniques of assistance to readers was put to test in this backroom assistance by proxy.

As far as I could I sought out the material by myself, visiting all the departments of the central library complex as necessary. The Great Hall of the Reference Library alone had 10,000 standard works immediately available for reference on the open shelves which encircled the seating and desks for 300 readers. The specialist staff on duty there, or somewhere below in the seven floors and their twenty-six miles of shelving, would help me if I had some particularly awkward enquiry.

Alternatively, I might find myself searching in one of the special collections, where I certainly needed assistance from the subject experts. There was the Lancashire Parish Register Society's Library; the Manchester Statistical Society's Library; The Lancashire Authors' Association Library; and many others, not forgetting the Commercial and Technical Libraries, in which I was, from past experience, more at home.

There was also the Henry Watson Music Library, with one of the largest collections of music and books about music in Europe. As with all special collections, its staff had to have a particular interest in and aptitude for their subject. Here one might find people borrowing twenty or more scores of Handel's *Messiah*, or something less well-known, for a local choir; or collecting band-parts for an orchestra. Others in the department might be studying books on the history or theory of music, the development of musical instruments—or even of famous orchestras: there is a complete set of Hallé Concert programmes just waiting for someone to write about the changing tastes of audiences.

Even so, there were occasions when our vast resources failed to provide the right book, and then I had to forward the request to the local office of the National Central Library. This is a co-operative organisation supported by most of the library services in the country, including some of the non-public ones, and through its agency libraries make special loans to one another, through special clearing houses known as Regional Bureaux, when local resources are inadequate. If necessary, the National Central Library will ask foreign libraries to lend items not otherwise available in this country—and, of course, British libraries will lend abroad in return when the need arises.

7

CROSSROADS

DURING MY TIME in charge of the Union Shelf Register I began to think more and more about my future career and to wonder how I ought to try and shape it. The easiest line of action was to carry on as I was and wait for someone else to make decisions for me.

The senior staff of the Manchester Public Libraries obviously thought that I had reasonable professional potentiality because I kept moving upwards, and always into attractive posts. There was every indication that I could expect further promotion later on, but, nevertheless, I felt uneasy. I was almost waiting for dead men's shoes and, after all, there were other keen young librarians on the Manchester staff. It we all stayed, then some of us were going to be unlucky.

If I applied for posts outside Manchester, even unsuccessfully, I was not allowing the grass to grow under my feet; and if I were successful, then I should gain not only promotion and further experience but experience in a different authority's service. When I look back I realise that I must have picked up this philosophy (the right one) at library school.

One can stagnate by staying too long in one system, even a very good one. A complete change encourages one to re-think one's attitudes. Good new ideas are forced into one's vision, and the debt can be repaid by clearing away any bad techniques one finds at the other end.

Furthermore, as I was to learn later on, to stay for too long with one authority during the early years of a career can be tantamount to committing professional suicide. No matter why one might stay: 'Because I enjoyed working there'; 'Because my wife did not wish to leave the district'; 'Because I did not wish to break up my social life in that town'; interviewing committees are prone to think such a person is unadventurous, or lacking in initiative, or even simply trying to cover up the fact that he has been applying for new posts for years without any success.

So it was with regret and almost a sense of doing Manchester a disservice that I began to look through the back pages of *The Times Literary Supplement* for suitable vacancies. Cynics in the profession will have it that these advertisement pages are the only ones we do read! What should I look for next? I had started in what was, in many ways, a university type library. Certainly Rylands had a strong academic background. To that experience I could now add four years in some of the most interesting departments of a large municipal system.

There were two possible directions in which I could look: to other large authorities, where I might expect to be engaged as a branch librarian or head of a section, or to smaller systems, where I might find myself in a position of considerable responsibility as co-ordinator of several facets of the library service. In each case the salary would be similar, for, in local government, the salary scales usually depend upon the size and wealth of the authority and not entirely upon the responsibilities involved.

For example, the Librarian-in-Charge of a large authority's branch library often receives the same salary as, say, a Deputy Borough Librarian working for a much smaller authority, yet the latter will have much more real responsibility. That may sound unfair, but it is a fact, and the only consolation lies in the bonus of experience gained by the person in the Deputy's post.

Another aspect of job-hunting, irrespective of profession, invites comparison with a lottery: one never knows whether a more advantageous position will be advertised next week or next month, and it is also never clear at the time whether a particular post will provide the right background for the unknown opportunities of the future.

One can only weigh the chances carefully before applying for, or accepting, a new job, bearing in mind the experiences of one's colleagues and learning from their mistakes or successes—as well as one's own, of course. Just as it can be short-sighted to stay in one place too long it can be equally bad to apply for another post within a very short time of a previous move. Both the present employer and the prospective employer will look askance at such a person.

There is also another important aspect of the search. Vacancies of the right kind may occur in neighbouring towns and villages, or they may occur miles away. The possibility of having to live away from home, in rooms or a flat, is not a slight one for the ambitious young librarian, and the expense of supporting one-self may well swallow up all the increase in pay. It is up to each individual to choose according to the circumstances. All that I am prepared to offer in the way of comment is that life itself is a series of partings.

I quickly suffered my first major disappointment and setback (as I saw it at the time) since my demobilisation. Manchester, like many other large cities, is surrounded by smaller places all within reasonable travelling time because of the vast network of trans-port facilities which exist in such areas. I read of an interesting vacancy in a nearby town with a small but good library service, and sent off my application knowing in all modesty that my experience to date was sound enough to make me an interesting possibility to the advertisers. I had also had a good grounding in the art of preparing an application, so I had few qualms on that account.

In the event I was never even called for an interview, and I was not only surprised but also very disappointed. I had been quite prepared for the eventuality of losing the post as a result of not interviewing well, or of being considered the wrong sort of person to work with the team I was hoping to join (personality affects one's chances at work as well as one's friendships), but I was rather shaken at not even being invited to attend for interview. The fact that nothing should be taken for granted takes a little getting used to.

About six months later, however, I was relieved beyond words, highly delighted, and telling everyone how lucky I had been not to get the post. Another, far more attractive, position became vacant when someone who had been a student with me at the Manchester Library School was appointed Deputy City Librarian of Salford. He had been Branch Librarian of Droylsden in the Lancashire County Libraries service, and I knew that Miss Cook, the County Librarian, gave every encouragement to enthusiastic librarians. This really was a post worth fighting for and, as I had not changed jobs recently, I could respectably put in an application for it. The salary was also considerably higher than the one I had missed.

It was one thing to send off my application; to think of my chances of success was something totally different. After all, Droylsden's reputation and the higher salary would attract a spate of applications, and on the previous occasion, when even I had thought that I stood a chance, I had been just an also-ran. I decided to try and forget all about it once my application had been posted.

Several weeks went by. Then I received a letter advising me that the post was being re-advertised because it had been decided to re-organise the Lancashire County branches into larger regional groups as opportunities presented themselves. The Branch Librarian at nearby Audenshaw was also about to retire, and so there would be a vacancy for an Area Librarian to administer the libraries of the two urban districts as a joint service.

The newly-created post would carry a commensurately higher salary—and my original application would be considered to refer to the new post! Well that really meant the end of my chances, I thought: the opposition now would be tremendous.

Just to make matters worse I then became ill with influenza and was confined to bed for about two weeks. As day followed day I began to worry: what if I was lucky enough to be called for an interview and yet was too ill to attend? The prospect was unbearable, and, sure enough, when I was beginning to shake off the worst of the illness, I did receive the invitation. Could I recover sufficiently to go? I had barely a week in which to get on to my feet again.

In fact I did manage to get to Droylsden, and sat awaiting my turn to go before the local Library Committee and the County Librarian. The longer I sat the more ill I began to feel, because I really had left my sick-bed too soon, but eventually it was my turn and I endeavoured to forget how awful I felt by concentrating upon what I was being asked by my inquisitors.

'Will you please relate to the Committee', the Chairman asked me, 'those aspects of your previous experience which you consider would be an asset in the post you are now seeking'. 'How would you go about amalgamating the two existing service areas?' 'How would you publicise the library's work?' And so on and on. After that I no longer cared about anything except getting back home to bed, but I had to wait until all the other applicants on the short list had been interviewed, and then for a little longer, while the Committee came to a decision. We all sat there, waiting.

Then, after what seemed like an eternity, the one thing happened that I had schooled myself not to think about. I was called back into the Committee Room and the Chairman addressed himself to me: 'Mr. Dearden, we have decided to offer you this new post. Are you willing to accept it?' What a moment! In the brief pause before one answers, what flashes across the mind? An almost indescribable feeling of relief, more than anything else; relief that one is not still out there in the waiting room feeling disconsolate. The joy, the satisfaction, come later.

On occasions people are offered a post and yet, for various reasons, they turn it down, but I definitely wanted this position, and said that I was delighted to accept it. There followed a few, brief, preliminary arrangements (the rest would be done by letter), and off I went to catch the bus home to my wife to tell her the good news. She has not been mentioned before in my story, but I had met her while we both were in the army, and we had married when I was Senior Assistant at Chorlton.

I was to report at my new library on 1st March 1951, and the waiting period of one month I found to be very much like a protracted hangover! Half the time I was glad and excited at the prospects of my new work; but half the time I was also very sad to be leaving behind the many friends I had made in the Manchester libraries. I knew that I should be meeting them again from time to time at professional meetings, but that was not quite the same as working with them. For me, these moves to new library authorities have always been bitter-sweet affairs, and I suppose that is the way it ought to be if one is lucky in the colleagues one finds.

8

COUNTY LIBRARY SERVICE

THOSE OF US who have been brought up in a town or city are sometimes puzzled by reference to a county library: in what way is it different from a public library? Is the former not open to the general public, perhaps? The short answer is that there is no difference in the concept of the service: both are public in the sense that they are rate supported and freely available to all who live within the boundaries of whichever local authority is responsible. County libraries serve all parts of a County except those towns, mostly large, which administer their own library services, and public library is the term which has been given by habit to those libraries administered by town and city councils.

Droylsden is an urban district just a few miles east of Manchester. Certain of its public services are organised by its own Urban District Council, but others, such as the police, fire, health, education and library services, are provided by the Lancashire County Council.

The library is quite pleasant. It was specially built for the purpose in 1937. When I took up my appointment there it had attached to it a smaller branch, also a new building, out at Waterloo, on the outskirts of Ashton-under-Lyne, and four village centres (tiny collections of books stored in boxes in school classrooms or church halls) which were run by volunteer unpaid local helpers on one evening each week.

Neighbouring Audenshaw was also to be my responsibility under the new arrangements, and two branches (one of them new, but the other no more than an inconvenient room in the council offices) served this scattered township. The total number of books available at all these service points was nearly 41,000; there were eleven of us on the combined staff; and there were about 47,000 people in our particular library area.

The immediate problem facing me upon appointment was that of unifying the previously separate services operated from Droylsden and from Audenshaw. Until this time they had had their own Librarian and staff, and each unit had offered a similar service, but in matters of organisational detail each had gone its own way, and the two staffs were not interchangeable, either. I wanted to draw up standard procedures for all the basic routine administrative tasks so that, in an emergency, any member of the staff could be sent to any one of the service points without the risk of not being sure what to do when they got there.

Furthermore, I wanted to build up a more varied stock in the area, to move books around in order to offer a changing selection and to create a union catalogue (a master catalogue) of the area stock in order to reduce our demands upon the headquarters', request service, thus speeding our local service to those whose requirements could not be met straight from the shelves.

I had explained my intention in general terms to the local Library Committee when I was interviewed for the post. These local committees are a feature of many County Library services and they are usually made up of local residents, councillors and laymen appointed to advise the County Council's Library Committee from the special advantage of their local knowledge.

Now I had the opportunity to discuss my plans in more detail with the Branch Supervisor. He was a well-known and greatly respected member of the profession (who was later to become State Librarian of Tasmania). Finally, I had to explain my intentions to the staff, for without their co-operation I could achieve nothing. Individuals had vital parts to play, and certain tasks had to be completed before any real changes could be made.

At this juncture the effect of habit and local conditions upon people's attitude to their work were made vividly clear to me. I had grown up in a large city. Once out of primary school, I had thought nothing of travelling several miles by tram to and from school each day. I had had to make a similar journey when I worked at the John Rylands Library, and again when I moved to the Manchester Central Library. It was an even longer journey for me to get to the Chorlton Branch from home, and I used a motor cycle to get to Droylsden.

However, some of the Droylsden and Audenshaw staff had never known this sort of life, and were inclined to resent any attempt on my part to cause them to be more mobile than had been necessary when first they began working for the County. The situation required tactful handling, because I had to have a team which was prepared to do a reasonable amount of travelling to and from the branches whenever necessary if my plans for co-ordination were to have any hope of success. I made it quite clear that, as far as possible, everyone would help to staff those branches or centres nearest to their homes, and with that undertaking the plan was put into operation.

As soon as possible I had to examine all the ways in which the routine tasks were carried out at the various places, draw up a standard instruction for the operation, and then make sure that all involved were quite clear about the new method. In this way I slowly compiled an instruction manual to which anyone could refer for guidance. It also had another use: it simplified the training of new staff later on by reducing the amount of verbal instruction they needed.

In these early days, too, in spite of all the work I wanted to get on with behind the scenes, I also made sure that I spent some time, at varying hours of the day, in the public part of the branches so that the readers and I could get to know each other.

Meeting all types of people who come into your library also stops you from becoming too solemn, but sometimes the smiles have to be hidden out of politeness. I had not been long at Droylsden when I was asked by an enquirer if I knew the address of Nellie Greenwood. I drew a blank in the local directory, and had to confess that, being a stranger to the district myself, I did not even know the lady, let alone her address (for I had the distinct impression that my enquirer thought I ought to). Nevertheless, I would ask my staff, for they all lived locally and might be more able to help.

Each was asked in turn, without success. In desperation I called up a much older temporary assistant who was working down in the basement. She was reputed to know a great many people. Up three flights of stairs she trudged. 'Do you know of a Nellie Greenwood?' I asked her. 'Oh, she is not called Greenwood now', interrupted my enquirer; 'she got married years ago, but I never did know her married name'. If that had happened in the kind of small Welsh town with which I am now familiar, everyone would have known Nellie's entire family history, and that of her cousins as well, but life is different over the border.

The biggest of all the jobs on my reconstruction programme was that of revising or editing the entire book stock of the area. A number of factors had caused my predecessors to defer this task, with the result that the shelves everywhere were cluttered with books that had ceased to warrant display space. There were out-of-date editions that needed to be replaced, either by a new edition of the same work, or by a completely new title on the same topic. Other works of specialised or seasonal interest needed to be grouped in a reserve stock down in the sub-basement store at Droylsden, but before I could do that I had to wait for the designated store-room to be shelved.

Once the extra shelving was ready I started to go through the entire stock, branch by branch and item by item, leaving piles of books behind me for complete withdrawal or transfer to our store after their catalogue cards had been removed from the catalogue cabinets by the staff. Then I had to choose more titles with which to re-stock the shelves. After that it was a relatively simple matter to keep a daily check on the books during the early morning tidying—and vary the stock content according to the time of year, as well as adding new works as they were published. It was then possible to start on the next improvement: a complete catalogue of the non-fiction stock of the area which would also show the location of each title—that is, whether or not there was a copy of a certain book at the Audenshaw Branch. the Littlemoss Centre, and so on, wherever it might be. This was a rather laborious task for the staff, but they persevered with it for an hour or two each day, as other work permitted, and eventually it was done.

After that I arranged for all the unsatisfied book requests we received to be sent direct to the main branch at Droylsden, where we checked to see if the books were at any of our other branches. If they were, we could collect them very quickly for use at the requesting branch; if not, we posted the requests on to the county headquarters at Preston for attention there. Thus we were making the fullest, organised, use of the local stock, and this meant, in many cases, a much quicker service to the readers.

When I was appointed I was told that we were to have an Area Children's Librarian on our staff. Her duties were to select and maintain the junior stock within the branches and centres; to arrange story hours for suitable times, when the children could listen to her telling or reading stories, to encourage them to borrow books and read them for themselves; to encourage school parties to visit us for instruction in how to use libraries; and to give advice, if required, on book selection and library management in some fifty neighbouring primary, junior and secondary modern schools.

This was no small task, but it was also a very stimulating and rewarding one. When she arrived, she, too, had to edit her stock, as I had done in the adult departments, then get to know and win the confidence of the younger library users, and also to make herself known to the local teachers.

Gradually we began to see the effects of her work. The children became more and more purposeful about their use of the library: they would use the catalogue to discover the whereabouts on the shelves of this or that category of books, just as they had been shown in the specially arranged classes on library usage, or to find what other titles we had by their favourite author of the moment. Often they became far more adept at using simple bibliographical aids than their parents, who had never had such opportunities when they were at school. Needless to say, our junior issues went up and up once this reorganisation got well under way.

The schools, too, were glad of specialist advice available for the asking. Most of them were very short of space, having been built long before school libraries were thought of, and in such places the books frequently had to be stored in boxes or trolley-like book cases that could be moved about. The newer schools were much better off, and our local secondary modern school had a magnificent purpose-built library that made many a public branch look inadequate. So the advice of the Children's Librarian had to be tailored at each place to what was possible within the local amenities.

Thus, whether through being in the library, or popping into schools, hundreds of children knew our Children's Librarian as a friend, and both they and everyone else were dismayed when she married and decided to retire from official life, leaving an enviable reputation to be lived up to by her successor.

Some years later we became one of the few libraries in the country to have a male Children's Librarian. He had joined our staff as a junior assistant, and his part-time studies for his Associate-ship had been interrupted by National Service with the Army, but, as soon as he could after qualifying, he concentrated on librarianship for children, and we were delighted to be able to offer him promotion when the present Children's Librarian resigned because her husband had obtained a post in another town.

While male librarians are quite prepared to emphasise the importance of work with children, few of them actually wish to specialise in it for long themselves, but this young man was different, and he slowly but surely became something of a legend in the area. Children would stop him on the street to talk about books, or ask him questions if they saw him on the local buses. At Christmas time he organised visits to the excellent special plays for children at the Manchester Library Theatre.

Eventually, and almost against his will, he was persuaded to inspire student librarians with his enthusiasm and expertise by accepting an appointment to lecture at the Manchester School of Librarianship. In many ways it was a shame to take him away from day to day librarianship, but we are very short, even now, of good children's librarians, and shorter still of people who can teach others how to fill the gap.

In such a busy area many activities must go on simultaneously. Every few months I had to meet the members of the local library committees to report on progress, or to provide them with technical information for the formulation of future policy. These committees also had the task of selecting new staff to fill the vacancies that occur in any system from time to time, and at all such meetings the Librarian acts as secretary and prepares the official minutes of the business transacted, as well as providing advice—which may or may not be accepted—as required.

There were also exhibitions to be planned and set up, for the better libraries try to become one of the cultural foci of a community by providing exhibitions and rooms which can be hired at little or no rent to local groups, such as the Workers' Educational Association or festival planning committees, which might not be able to exist if they had to pay commercial rentals for such accommodation.

Each year we used to have an exhibition of paintings and drawings done by the children in our local schools. The head teachers had to be informed well in advance and invited to support us with entries. Then we had to find someone to make the final selection, for we always received more material than we could use. Finally, a day or two before the opening of the exhibition, the exhibits had to be hung on special display stands, and that was rather like doing a huge jig-saw puzzle, simplified to the extent that it had rectangular pieces, but with the pattern having to be made up as one went along.

Usually we also staged a similar event for adult artists, as well as providing the same facilities for the annual exhibition of the Droylsden Photographic Society. Most of these events were officially opened, perhaps by some local dignitary such as the Chairman of the Council, in the evening, when the greatest number of people were likely to be free to attend, and usually this meant an extra evening duty for me in order to look after our guests and make them feel welcome.

In between the large exhibitions there were smaller displays on matters like fine printing, book illustration, or early editions of the Bible—the latter being arranged to coincide with a Bible Week organised by the churches in the district. Nor was that all. We were there, primarily, to lend books and supply information to the public, so, amid the book stock, we arranged small displays featuring books on topical subjects to encourage some of the readers to consider borrowing items they might otherwise have missed.

We would bring together books for gardeners and those about stately homes and architecture, to suggest new aspects of visits to National Trust and similar properties. The use of atomic power for peaceful purposes was another topic. Important events in some part of the world would be spotlighted by a display of books covering the scenery, customs, history and politics of the countries involved. Normally, all these books would be scattered throughout the library because of their basic classification—under gardening, architecture, politics, geography, and so on.

We had on the staff a very talented assistant who not only enjoyed building new displays, but was also very good at lettering and painting, and his work always had a strong visual impact. Some libraries employ a professional display artist at head-quarters to prepare material for use at each of several branches in turn, but our good fortune meant that we could do more or less what we wanted to suit local convenience.

Gradually, too, I was able to take some account of our service to groups of people outside the library. As I became better known I began to receive invitations to speak at meetings of parent-teacher associations or church groups. Such contacts are extremely important opportunities to explain our service to people with only a hazy idea of what the modern public library has to offer: in the past, many librarians have been their own worst enemies in that they have failed to publicise either themselves or their libraries adequately.

These occasions gave me a chance to meet and talk to those who might otherwise have remained strangers, and though serious in intent they were not without their humour, even if, sometimes, it was unconscious. There was, for example, the afternoon our Superintendent of Branches was invited to a Women's Fellowship meeting in a village near Preston. He arrived at the church hall and was introduced to the lady who was to be chairman. 'How long shall I talk for?' he asked. 'Oh, until you hear a hissing sound', came the unexpected reply. He had experienced some rather informal meetings in his time, but nobody had ever hissed at him, yet here was someone telling him to expect it. He was rather alarmed. 'Yes', the lady went on, 'that will mean the geyser is boiling and it is time for a cup of tea'.

Also, for a time, I found myself on more than a nodding acquaintanceship with the local police force. One Monday morning I arrived at the library to find the caretaker thoroughly excited. During the weekend we had been burgled. At such a moment all one's reading of detective stories takes on a new significance. 'Don't touch anything', I said, 'the police will want to look for finger prints'.

My instruction made it rather a problem as to how we should send for the police, but the more I looked at the tiny window pane which the thieves had broken to gain entry, the more I considered it likely that we were dealing with young children, so I decided that they had probably not had a telephone conversation with friends during their raid. Thus I did not bother to wrap my handkerchief around the instrument in the approved manner.

The detectives were on the scene very quickly. A jumble of fingerprints was found on a cash box which had contained about five shillings, but that was only to be expected: all the staff handled the cash box from time to time. The search had to be narrowed down. 'Would we mind having our fingerprints taken?' we were asked. Out came the ink pads and special sheets of paper. Fingers and thumbs were rolled in the ink and pressed one by one onto the records, each with one of our names on the top. Then away went the detectives, taking the cash box with them.

A strange set of prints was found on the box, but they did not match with any already known to the police, so they did not afford any clue to the identity of the thief. Nor was he ever found, but three times in about five weeks were there similar break-ins, each one causing more expense in broken windows and forced doors and desks than the value of the money stolen. In the end police officers hid in the library for several weekends in succession, but our burglars had moved to pastures new. At least they never bothered us again, and some time later the police returned to us our fingerprint records: under law only the prints of convicted persons may be retained.

Good library authorities make provision for staff to receive what is often referred to as in-service training. Generally this is for junior staff, so that they may discuss matters of policy and procedure in relation to their own tasks, and so understand more clearly the full extent of the service that a properly trained assistant can offer to the public. Some authorities also arrange conferences for senior staff to allow them the opportunity, once in a while, of sitting back to take a careful look at new developments in library science with a view to adapting them to their own service.

In Lancashire the branch libraries used to send their newest juniors to a larger branch within easy travelling distance for a weekly meeting organised by the Superintendent of Branches. Droylsden was one such centre, and the programme of talks, demonstrations and discussions covered matters such as how to deal with complaints (even good services cannot escape the occasional one, and staff must remain polite no matter how badly they are provoked), display techniques, work with children, the technical information section at the headquarters library, and so on.

The social side was not overlooked, either. We had a Staff Guild which arranged two or three meetings each year, usually on a Sunday, when staff from all over the county could meet each other and listen to some interesting speaker, perhaps a local author, like John Braine or Robert Neill, or a broadcaster. Eventually I found myself elected Chairman one year, and then it was my pleasant duty to help organise the meetings, and look after and introduce our speakers. We also had an annual country house party, when we hired a former stately mansion and spent a full weekend in some delightful part of the countryside. Wives and friends were equally sure of enjoying these occasions.

9

PROFESSIONAL ASSOCIATIONS

THE LIBRARY ASSOCIATION has been mentioned already in connection with the professional qualifications. However, it is not the only association for those concerned with librarianship in this country. Industrial or special librarians may be members of Aslib: the Association of Special Libraries and Information Bureaux, or they may join the Institute of Information Scientists —a more recent foundation. Then there is the School Libraries Association, catering especially for teachers who are in charge of school libraries. Each institution arranges meetings and conferences for members.

As a member of the Library Association I was free to attend the meetings arranged by the Branch Committee for the North-western part of the country. They were held by invitation of a local library committee, and time was always made in the programme to inspect some aspect of the local library service: a new or modernised branch library, perhaps; an important collection of books recently left to a library; a newly-formed gramophone record library; an extension to the reference library. Thus one could see what other authorities were doing and get new ideas for the future.

Library Association members also divide themselves into groups interested in particular aspects of librarianship, and hold special meetings devoted to such topics as county library work; library service to young people; university, college and research libraries; or reference and special libraries.

Assistant librarians, that is, all librarians except chiefs of systems, have yet another grouping within the Library Association: an Association of Assistant Librarians (the A.A.L.), a most useful platform whereon all below the rank of Chief Librarian may have their say, and practise public speaking without the embarrassment of being watched by very senior librarians. The subjects chosen for A.A.L. meetings, too, are selected for their interest to the rank and file.

As often as I could, I had attended such meetings ever since my return from the Army in 1947. Some took place during the day, when I was allowed time off from work; others were held in the evenings, when one attended in one's own time. After a while, one of the A.A.L. officials, always ready to encourage newcomers to take an even more active part in things, asked me if I would be prepared to propose or second votes of thanks to some of the speakers, and I had the sense to say yes. Looking back, it was probably because I had not the nerve to say no. Whatever the reason, it was this sort of experience that made it easier for me later, when I had to address groups of people at Droylsden.

The final outcome of my interest and activity in A.A.L. affairs came, nevertheless, as a great surprise. During my stay at Droylsden I was persuaded by some of the Committee members to stand at the next annual election, and, to my amazement, I secured enough votes and joined the Committee in 1951. We used to meet at about monthly intervals to plan future programmes: discussing possible topics, deciding which speakers to approach, and whereabouts in the area to locate our meetings— always supposing that we could arrange the necessary invitations.

Sometimes the meetings would be devoted to a paper delivered by someone from our own area; sometimes we would invite an important person in the profession from further afield. Other programmes would take the form of a debate or a discussion— with a panel of celebrities on the platform. We also arranged revision schools at weekends near examination time, for, in those days, many of our members were still studying part-time for their qualifications.

The sequel to one committee meeting in particular was less rewarding. It had been a long yet fruitful evening, but eventually our discussions came to an end and, at peace with the world, I rode out of Manchester on my motor cycle. Soon I was going along the Cheshire lanes, with not another vehicle in sight, for the time was about 11.30 p.m. I had a powerful machine, but I was in no great hurry to reach home, for it was a glorious night, and when a car's headlamps behind me suggested that the driver wished to overtake me I had no objection. In fact I politely waved him on.

The car roared past and stopped in front of me. An illuminated red sign flashed the words, 'Stop. Police'. My speed had varied between 39 and 44 m.p.h. over half a mile, I was told, and I would be reported. The summons came as a Christmas present on the 23rd December, and subsequently I was two guineas poorer, but what hurt most was the fact that I could hardly tell the police that I had not been really trying at the time.

At the end of my first year on the A.A.L. Committee there was another surprise in store for me. One of the Senior Committee members telephoned one day to persuade me to accept nomination as Honorary Secretary to the Committee: the current Secretary had announced that other committments would prevent him from continuing in office.

The possibility of my stepping into his shoes had never occurred to me, but apparently the rest of the Committee had discussed this informally, and had decided that I should be approached. The prospect was an attractive one, but I was not sure that I could spare the time, either, so I asked for a little while in which to think things over: I did not wish to accept and then do the work badly because I could not devote sufficient time to it.

In the end I decided to let matters take their own course: I accepted this second nomination and was again successful to the extent of being returned unopposed. I also bade goodbye to most of the remainder of my spare time, for I was still studying part-time to complete my final examinations for a Fellowship of the Library Association. (Nowadays, one produces a thesis for the Fellowship).

The honorary secretary of any organisation is the memory, typist, correspondent and general agent for the whole committee. The committee members make the decisions (the chairman keeping everyone in order), but in the end it is the secretary who sends out copies of the agenda to summon members to meetings, records and circulates the minutes, and makes all the arrangements —by telephone or letter—to bring into fruition all the decisions taken by his committee.

There is no room for laziness or slip-shod work: this would only result in loss of confidence in the committee if members at large were notified of events too late to make arrangements to attend them, or if an invited speaker made a long journey to our area only to find that no one had thought to meet him at the station and pilot him to the scene of the meeting.

I had to keep in close touch with the Chairman in between committee meetings, for he was empowered to take limited action on behalf of the full committee at all times when a decision was required too urgently to allow of its discussion with the rest of the committee. Once our programme of meetings had been arranged I had to make the final critical plans with the librarians who were providing the hospitality, and now it was my responsibility to find volunteers to thank the speakers and our hosts at the end.

It was all very absorbing work, but at times it could also be rather hair-raising as dead-lines approached, and a series of unconnected accidents might make it seem very unlikely that our programme would go as advertised. There was the Sunday we arranged a coach visit from Manchester to see Fountains Abbey and Harewood House. Apart from the library, which we would

see as part of the normal guided tour of the house, there was
nothing vaguely professional about this excursion: it was purely
a social occasion, arranged for the Spring.

The event was advertised around the libraries, and enough
members and their friends announced their intention of coming
along, so we duly hired a private coach to take us all. 'Could the
coach operator advise us of a suitable stop for lunch?' I asked.
There would be no problem about that, I was assured: it was
simply a matter of asking the driver before we set off. He would
know of several places, but it would be worth our while to make
a telephone booking before we left, because thirty-odd lunches
at once might be a tall order out of the normal holiday season.

The Sunday morning dawned bright and clear. Even the coach
arrived on time to pick us up from an otherwise deserted St
Peter's Square. We mentioned our lunch problem to the driver.
He was not the normal excursion driver, we were told; the
regular driver was ill, and our man knew of only one place where
we might eat. When I telephoned the restaurant it was closed,
so we had to rearrange our itinerary and call at Harewood
House first, because there we could obtain light refreshments in a
coach house buffet, or more expensive meals in the village at the
Harewood Arms. The change of plan was announced with no
indication of the chaos so narrowly avoided, and with sighs of
relief we began to enjoy ourselves with the rest.

Thus our committee looked after the area around Manchester;
similar committees being responsible for other parts of the
country. All the district committees nominated two representatives (generally the Chairman and Secretary) to speak for them
on a national level in the meetings of the A.A.L. Council at the
Library Association headquarters in London. This Council
usually met about six times a year; its business lasted a full
working day on each occasion, and it was therefore necessary
for delegates to travel up to London on the day before and stay
overnight. Expenses for such business trips are met by the Library

Association, and good library authorities will allow the delegates time off from their duties.

There came a time in 1957 when, as Chairman of the Manchester and District Committee for that year, I made the first journey of the new year with the Honorary Secretary, a girl from one of the Manchester branch libraries who had taken over that office from me. Both of us were familiar with London, having visited the capital on a number of previous occasions, but never before had we gone as a team, and events were to make the occasion a truly memorable one.

The journey from Manchester passed without incident, and after dinner we went to a theatre to round off the day. It was all very pleasant. Next morning found us strolling down Tottenham Court Road to the Library Association building, and, as we were passing Heal's store, we realised that we had about twenty minutes to spare, so we decided to make a short detour.

We browsed around the shop, and then, mindful of the time, we retraced our steps to the door. Like a true gentleman, I opened it to allow my companion to precede me, but courtesy, it would seem, does not always pay. As I was about to follow, something in the shop distracted my attention for a moment, but my gaze was quickly drawn back to the street outside by a horrible crack as the head of our brand new Secretary hit the pavement—and there she was, lying flat on her back. A student, with less spare time than we, had run straight into her as she left the shop doorway, which was slightly masked by two flanking columns.

For a moment she lay there stunned before she was assisted back into Heal's, where kindly staff made her comfortable until she had recovered somewhat. Then a taxi was called: a hospital check-up seemed advisable, and for the rest of that morning I steered her, not around committee rooms, but—in a wheel-chair—from casualty ward to X-ray department of the Middlesex Hospital.

Once it was certain that no serious damage had been done, the houseman who examined her voiced his amusement: 'You are the first casualty ever to be brought in after being knocked down by a moving pedestrian', he chuckled. Twelve years later that misguided soul still speaks to me on occasion. She also claims that she still has a lump on her head, but it must be a bump of knowledge, for now she is a senior lecturer on the staff of a large library school.

A.A.L. Council Meetings do not usually suffer from such dramatic interruptions. The representatives gather to discuss all professional matters relating to the welfare of assistant librarians, from educational opportunities and the publishing of suitable text books to a consideration of new subscription rates.

In this committee work at local and national levels the members obtain valuable experience in convincing others of the soundness of their ideas by means of reasoned argument; experience that will stand them in good stead when faced by politically experienced councillors in their own library committees later on, and many of those I first met at such meetings are now chiefs of important library systems. As such they are not allowed to hold office in the Association of Assistant Librarians, but you will find a number of them have been entrusted with even more power, having been voted onto the Council of the Library Association itself.

IO

THE SHAPE OF THINGS TO COME

In 1956, while still at Droylsden, I passed the last of my Finals and obtained my Fellowship of the Library Association. A month or two later the Head of the Manchester School of Librarianship asked me if I would like to do some part-time teaching for him: the school had grown in size, and he needed someone to lecture in bibliography up to Registration (A.L.A.) level.

I did not realise it at the time, but this unsolicited compliment was going to play a very important part in the shaping of my future career: it was to interest me in an aspect of librarianship that developed out of all recognition in the next ten years, but in 1956 only a relative few could see what lay ahead.

Over the last four or five years I had transformed the independant branch staffs of the Droylsden-Audenshaw area into a well-organised team which needed the minimum of supervision. The book-stock had been carefully edited and built up so that readers had plenty of up-to-date books from which to choose. Certainly the pressure was off me in that direction, and I could afford to consider other responsibilities.

I was still on the Manchester and District Committee of the A.A.L., but that was not as demanding as the office of Honorary Secretary had been. The lecturing would have to be done in the daytime, and therefore my day off would have to be arranged to coincide with the school's timetable, but that was no great problem, either.

The factor that concerned me most was the amount of time I should need to spend on lecture preparation, for it is one thing to be knowledgeable about a subject; it is another to be able to explain its complexities to students for three-quarters of an hour at a time without leaving something out that the lecturer takes for granted, or failing to reach a satisfactory point of conclusion. I should be required to lecture for a whole morning: being a part-time (or visiting) lecturer meant that I could not spread my four lectures over a longer period.

I had done some teaching in the Army, when I was attached to the Education Corps for the last few months before my demobilisation; and, as I had found it stimulating then, I decided to accept this new proposal.

Work on my lecture notes had to start at once. Then the actual course started, and I was hard pressed to produce enough new material in time for each successive lecture. Remember: I was also working a librarian's normal 38-hour week, which entailed two late evening duties and my share of the Saturday afternoon rota. Any library or A.A.L. committee meetings also made further inroads on my free evenings.

It was hard work, but I found that I enjoyed teaching students about printing, book illustration, binding and analytical bibliography, so it all seemed very much worth while the effort. Even more to the point, the examination results at the end of the session were above the national average, so I could feel that the students had also gained from my enjoyment: a most important consideration.

Not unreasonably, I was very tired at the end of that academic year. There was the long summer vacation in which I could recuperate: I should have only my normal week's work to do during that time! And my own summer holidays lay ahead. 'Next winter it will not be half so tiring', I thought: I should need only to brush up my existing lecture notes and add anything new that was likely to be of importance.

Then I had another surprise. The Head of the Library School asked if I could also take over responsibility for half of the

Finals Bibliography course, sharing it with himself. That took up the other half of my day off, and it was a case of going back to high-pressure lecture preparation all over again. There were only eight students taking the Final Bibliography paper at Manchester during the 1957–58 session, but they were very keen.

Seven of them passed the examination at the end of the course —the other went into hospital with acute appendicitis! Strange to relate, one of those seven is now a fellow lecturer in my own college. Another is Deputy City Librarian of Southampton, and the one lacking his appendix is Librarian of a northern College of Art and the author of a book on a Victorian worthy.

The year 1957 was also important for the profession at large. It was then that the Ministry of Education issued its *Circular No. 322* to encourage local authorities to set up or extend libraries in their colleges of further education, sometimes referred to as technical colleges. In most colleges this meant pioneering from scratch, creating brand new libraries specially orientated towards teaching students how to use books efficiently. This latter had never been thought of before, not even in the universities, and my newly awakened interest in teaching made me very sensitive to the possibilities.

I was also very much aware of the dangers of staying at Droylsden much longer. In fact I had been there too long already for my own professional good, and I have been told that the chairman of one of the authorities to whom I applied for a post about that time said as much when speaking against my appointment, which I dearly wanted.

So I was stirred into a very serious hunt for another post. Also, to be fair to myself, I had begun to realise that I had done as much as one person could for branch libraries in my area. Everything was ticking over too smoothly for the work to present a challenge any longer: my successes as an organiser were making life too simple for me. Someone else might find other things to do, but I needed to move on.

I began to apply for any post on a higher salary that offered an extension to my experience, and to which, at the same time, I could also offer something from my own past work and training. Very often I received an invitation to present myself for interview, but, equally often, there was always someone else on the short-list who was just that little better than I was, or whose personality was more pleasing to the interviewers than was mine, or who was simply a woman being interviewed by a woman chief officer who did not wish to employ a man if she could help it.

These are all fair reasons for anyone not being successful in an interview, but one must be sure to remember that they are three different valid reasons. The converse of the third reason is, of course, equally true and valid if the applicant is female. In the majority of cases, however, the stumbling block is not whether an applicant is a man or a woman, but whether they are likely to do the job well.

Nevertheless, these rejections made me more and more depressed. I even began to dread finding an attractive advertisement: 'I shall get an interview', I used to think, 'but someone else will be offered the job. Why bother to apply?' The crisis really came when I saw a new post advertised by Reading Technical College.

The task and the situation of Reading in the Thames valley both attracted me, but I dillied and dallied for day after day, always putting off the actual preparation of my application until tomorrow and knowing very well, secretly, that I had not the heart to do anything positive.

I had come to the conclusion that I was stuck. I can still remember that the closing date for applications was a Monday. On the previous Friday I had still done nothing about applying. Just before 8 p.m. (I was working late on that day) the telephone rang; it was my wife, who, with a very few well-chosen words, stung me into agreeing to do something positive before I left for home.

After the library had closed for business my wife rang again to dictate from my file at home the relevant facts and figures which I needed for my application—as the years and jobs go by one gets too hazy for accuracy about movements in a varied career. I typed out the document, posted it at the main post office for safety, and went home in a bad temper.

I was called for interview. I obtained the post, and I have never ceased to be grateful to my wife. One should never, never give up.

I I

CREATING A COLLEGE LIBRARY

MY APPOINTMENT as Librarian of the Reading Technical College
was effective from 1st April 1959. This would be All Fools Day,
I was reminded. Some of the less well-informed members of the
staff there thought it a most appropriate occasion on which to
start something as odd as a college library: they had managed
very well without one for years. But, fortunately for me, that
was not the Principal's belief, and his support, and that of many
of the senior staff, including a most useful ally and valuable
friend—the Registrar, turned a difficult job into a very rewarding
experience.

A move to another district brings with it problems totally
unconnected with the work. First and foremost there is accommodation to consider. Flats are not too difficult to obtain, and
one can always make do with a bedsitter as a temporary base if
one is single, and thus seek out something more permanent at
leisure when one knows the new district better. A family move
is far more complicated.

There is a new house to be found—at the right price, suitable
for the family requirements, in the right situation, and with the
minimum of delay. Getting all those variables to coincide can
be a very trying business. Then one has to sell the old house
—as soon as possible, and at the best possible price. The further
one is away from one's old home, the harder it is to make joint
decisions with one's wife—who has a right to an equal share in
choosing where next she is going to live.

It is quite easy to lose the chance of buying a particular house simply through waiting until one's wife can travel up to inspect the property. On the other hand, it is possible to find something very quickly, and to complete the removal from one house to the other within the few weeks it usually takes to terminate the old contract of employment.

In our case we found a house without too much difficulty, but it was not due for completion for eight months. I therefore lived on my own in Reading; we sold our house in Cheshire; and my wife and baby daughter stayed at Lowestoft with relations. The furniture was put into store—more expense.

As my new salary was only about £60 a year greater than my old one, and as house prices in the south of England are considerably higher than those in the north, there was very little to spare for weekend visits to see my family. However, we well knew that a move was essential for my career and, as we both wanted to move south, we had to trust that the expense would be worth it all in the end. Events have since shown that we chose right.

What we did not foresee at the time was the chaos of our eventual move into the newly-built house. One bleak November day I supervised the delivery of our furniture from store, and then set off to collect my family from Lowestoft. About three and a half hours later, in the darkness, I skidded off the road at a very awkward corner in the wilds of Suffolk. Fortunately I missed two massive trees as I rolled through the hedge, but the car ended upside down in a field with me unconscious inside it—and I was still thirty-odd miles from my destination.

The car was very badly damaged. My injuries, apart from slight concussion, were restricted to a few grazes, but I still had to spend three days in bed, and was fit for very little when at last we were all transported back to Reading in a hired car.

Prior to my appointment as the first Librarian of the College a small number of books had been accumulated in each department of the College, and these had been stored in the various departmental offices and staff rooms. They were used mainly by the staff, and a few technical journals also circulated among the staff in a very haphazard manner. There was nowhere where students could sit down to read and use books as they practised using tools and scientific apparatus in the workshops and laboratories. Somehow, I had to change all that.

In theory, the books and periodicals already in the College were to be transferred to my care forthwith, but I made it quite clear that I was not going to exercise my option overnight, and those who had never relished having what were regarded as their books taken from them were convinced that they had won the first round.

In fact, I had nowhere to store the books if I had taken them, and a glance around had shown me that some were no longer worth taking away in any case, because they were out of date. Only the chemists, the physicists and the printers had built up good basic collections, and the lecturers responsible had assured me that they would be delighted to hand everything over to my care as soon as I was ready.

First of all I had to arrange for the conversion of the large lecture room which was to become the library. When I arrived it was full of stored furniture, and had an elaborately fitted shop window at one end. I discussed with the Maintenance Engineer what might be achieved; the carpenters were sent for; the big refit began. Meanwhile I rigged up a trestle table as a temporary desk in one corner, tried not to be put off by all the jumble around me, and began ordering all the equipment I needed—from a wastepaper basket upwards.

At the other end of the room the carpenters sawed and planed away as they gradually assembled the wooden shelving. The plate glass of the shop window was fronted with book shelves; the fittings behind it were ripped out and the space turned into a small store room and an office for me. Then I retreated into it while the rest of the library was completed, but it often seemed as if the work would never be finished.

It was a most difficult time. I could sense that some of the staff were plainly waiting for me to perform a miracle overnight, and that they were rather baffled when I did no such thing. Others were just frankly curious as to what I could do under the rather daunting circumstances. All the time there were questions, over coffee or during lunch; and I would describe over and over again what the eventual library service would be like: the intended size of the book stock; the way it would be arranged; how many books I would allow people to have on loan at any one time; what would happen about overdue loans; book selection methods; and so on.

Through it all I had to be very patient because, at that stage, I had no way of convincing anyone that I could do it, and I knew that the only sure way of convincing my new colleagues was by deeds, not words. Yet for weeks, while the carpenters worked, I personally could see very little for my efforts.

Fortunately for me, the Principal had known similar frustrations as he had waited for his college to be built not so many years before. He never made me feel uncomfortable because I had as yet few visible results. He kept himself informed of progress without ostentation, and when he did make an official visit he always left me feeling that, perhaps after all, I was making more progress than I realised. In short, he was an excellent morale booster.

By degrees it became possible to arrange my newly-purchased equipment so that I could use it. My first book orders arrived, and I was able to begin cataloguing and classifying the books as they were received. Of one thing I was certain: I must keep everything flowing through a processing sequence. Once I allowed books to arrive faster than I could process them there would be chaos.

It was very tempting to get new books into the library by the thousand without arranging them in a useful classified order, on the pretext of being able to sort things out later, but I knew that such delusion was pointless and so I made haste slowly but surely. I wanted to build a library, not an apology for one, so I had to produce something more than a collection of books.

I was handicapped by the fact that I had no assistance, clerical or professional, at this stage, so I had to be a jack-of-all-trades, doing a little of everything in turn to keep things moving, but it did mean that the build-up was slower than I liked, and slower than it need have been if the local education authority had made provision for an adequate supporting staff. As it was, when I was typing catalogue cards, for example, I must have been the highest paid typist in Berkshire. The office typists had more work than they could attend to without delay, so it was unreasonable to burden them further.

Such under-staffing is still a feature of some college libraries, I fear, because many of the people who govern the colleges still fail to understand that there is more work involved than in a branch library of similar size, which is always supported by headquarters' staff behind the scenes. Nevertheless, I would not hesitate to recommend the life to any really professionally-minded young librarian.

A considerable amount of the missionary work among local further education office staffs has now been done; the inspectors of the Department of Education and Science are helping enormously, too, with advice and encouragement. The climate is right for further development in this field, and college libraries will be needing many more professionals on their staffs.

In the creation of such a new library the selection of stock is a particular challenge: it is not just a question of what to buy on this or that subject, but of what to buy first. I sought to create a small basic collection for each of the departments by purchasing reference and standard works not already in the college, together with new editions of works represented in the departmental stocks only by superseded editions. I also obtained as quickly as possible the encyclopaedias, dictionaries and yearbooks without which no library is complete.

When people speak of such general reference works they automatically think of something like the *Encyclopaedia Britannica* or *Chambers's Encyclopaedia* on the one hand, and the Oxford dictionaries on the other, but the librarian must remember the more specialised ones as well. There are encyclopaedias dealing with just one subject, like physics, chemistry, photography, building, or automobile engineering. Dictionaries of foreign languages are also vital.

Of similar necessity, if I was to be able to offer a really professional information service to the teaching staff, were sets of the book trade and national bibliographies. Even subject experts forget or only half remember the exact details of some books to which they suddenly need to refer, or else they explain that they would like the library to have some books on a new aspect of college work, and ask what there is for them to choose from.

Only in a few of the big cities can one go into a really well-stocked book shop and make a selection from copies waiting on the shelves. But I could check for the exact title, publisher and price when necessary, or draw up a list of suggestions which our local bookseller was always prepared to obtain on approval so that we could select the most relevant items for purchase.

Similarly I needed lists of films and other audio-visual aids to teaching, because the concept of library service has long since been extended beyond the provision of printed or written materials alone. In a college it may not be desirable to store in the library what are simply teaching aids, but the librarian is best able to keep a record of what is available.

Once I had these initial tasks under control I had time to keep abreast of current publications. I had to familiarise myself with every aspect of all the teaching done in the college: at what level of scholastic ability did each course start, and to what level did each rise? Without such understanding I could not begin to make any choice from the many similar-sounding titles in the lists that daily reached my desk.

Selection for any special library is much more complex than that for a public library stock, for, although the subject interests of the former are restricted to carefully defined areas and degrees of scholarship, the specialists' needs create individual limitations which are generally more inhibiting than the pervasive nature of a public library service.

Book reviews, as in any branch of librarianship, are a tremendous help when making a choice, and most technical and scientific journals provide assistance in this respect. I also enlisted the co-operation of the teaching staff from time to time. After all, they knew how they wanted to teach their subjects; they might also prefer one author's approach to another's.

Here again, the sensible solution was to obtain the books on approval and make a final choice only after examination of the texts. Not infrequently I found myself drawing attention to new books whose existence was still unknown to a lecturer: teaching and marking work often leave little time for catching up with new publications except during the vacation.

As day followed day the stock gradually began to increase not only in quantity but also in usefulness, and as this happened the teaching staff began to see that the intentions of the Principal and my promises were really producing something that should have been in the college from its foundation. To be fair to everyone, prior to my arrival no one had been allowed to buy books at the rate I was doing. No one had had the funds, but now there was a larger monetary vote for books, and I was showing what could be done with it, and the idea caught on.

It was at last safe to begin transferring the departmental collections into the library so that they could be catalogued and amalgamated with my new stock. In some cases I had already bought more on their subject than I was taking over from a department, but two collections were very good—as I had noticed earlier on—and the staff responsible for having built them up were eager to have the new library service in operation as quickly as possible. With them I could begin straight away to consider how best we might widen their excellent basic stocks.

All this naturally took several months to work out. Things moved faster once I had my own clerical assistant, but even so I was grateful for the Principal's decision not to allow unlimited access by the students until the new session opened in September. Staff usage during this interim period did not pose the problem that an influx of hundreds of students would have done.

Right from the beginning I had been warned that my library accommodation was only of a temporary nature, and for that knowledge I was glad, for the space we had—though better than nothing—was grossly inadequate. It was hoped that government approval for a college extension, including a large library, was not far off, so anything that I ordered in the form of special library fitments had to be designed with the future building in mind to avoid wasting our money.

Particularly affected were the periodicals. I took out new subscriptions to widen our range of technical journals, and, for their display, I had made special adaptations of racks which had first caught my attention in the library of the Manchester College of Science and Technology. Each unit contained a vertical series of shelves at intervals of about three inches, and upon these the journals lay together with some of the previous issues, the name of the periodical being lettered on each shelf.

With these there was no fear of wasting yards of wall space as the conventional display fittings tend to do. They were also capable of being arranged in groups, so I was not likely to embarrass the design of the future library by any inflexibility.

Another basic matter had given me much food for thought: the choice of methods for keeping record of book issues. For a number of reasons I felt that the standard system as used in most public lending libraries and involving the production of borrowers' tickets was not entirely suitable for our library.

I wanted a more ambitious method which would obviate the clerical work of making out readers' tickets, for, in the foreseeable future, I was not likely to have anything approaching the public library proportion of staff to borrowers. During a visit to the magnificent library serving the Atomic Weapons Research Establishment at nearby Aldermaston I found the very thing I was looking for.

Pads of specially printed loan request forms are held in a special dispenser which interleaves the forms with carbon paper. Completion of the top copy with details of the author and title of the book, plus the borrower's name and department within the college, produces four or five copies as well. These are enough for the same information to be filed in several different sequences to show which books are on loan to which people, what books are held by a certain individual, which books are due back on a given date, and still leave one to spare for sending off as a reminder if a book becomes overdue.

The system was not without snags of its own making, but the advantages far outweighed them in my estimation. Later, as other college librarians heard of my adoption of this issue system, I was inundated with requests for further information.

With the approach of autumn and the new academic year I was as ready for opening the library fully as one could be under the circumstances. Posters advertising the new service were displayed in prominent positions throughout the college, and the teaching staff were asked to make special mention of it in their opening lectures.

Quickly a satisfactory number of students began to use the library, not only to borrow books from it, but also to read and to write up notes within its quiet atmosphere. Even so, it was my special duty to ensure that all students were not only aware of the facilities but fully conversant with their proper use.

This is what makes college librarianship different from other branches of the profession: there is a strong teaching element involved. In the case of the technical college the books and periodicals are shown to be an extension of the other workshop and laboratory equipment, the spanners, screwdrivers, lathes, oscilloscopes, retorts and bunsen burners that the technologist already takes for granted. He expects the lecturer in chemistry or engineering to give instruction in how to make full use of the latter; the tutor-librarian has to provide instruction in how to make the most of the former.

It was one thing, however, to demonstrate the sense of this to my lecturing colleagues; it was another to persuade them to allocate some of their time to me, for their complaint was always that the syllabus grew longer, yet the number of teaching hours in an academic year never increased. The ability to bargain and convince other people is a hidden feature of librarianship, but the most successful librarians have something of the good sales-man in their professional make-up, and the tutor-librarian has also to develop a flair for teaching and encouraging even unwilling craft apprentices to use books.

This teaching may be formal classroom work, or it may be of an informal nature in the library, as students look for a certain piece of information, but it does result in the identification of the library and its staff as a special place in the college: a store house of information always available for the seeking.

The students in such colleges of further education (a term that embraces technical colleges, colleges of technology, colleges of commerce and colleges of art) are studying a very wide range of subjects at many different levels. Some may be taking 'A' level subjects not offered in the schools which they had attended previously; some may even be trying to improve on their old school 'A' level results in the same subjects. Others may be on a day's leave of absence from work each week to study technical and craft subjects such as printing, photography, welding, brick-laying, electronics, plumbing, automobile engineering, or commercial and managerial topics—economics, personnel management, accountancy, commercial art and window-dressing. There may well be similar courses for other students to attend full-time.

All are working to satisfy the educational requirements of a variety of professional bodies in order to obtain City and Guilds certificates, university entrance, or Associateships of the many institutions for Architects, Townplanners, Electrical and Mechanical Engineers, Chemists, Physicists, Accountants and Public Administrators, to name only a few. Some of the colleges also offer courses in preparation for external degrees of London University.

The academic ability of the students therefore varies enormously within any one college. So does the age of these people: from school-leavers to those in executive positions who are seeking extra qualifications. Most of them come from the immediate neighbourhood; others travel by car, train or bus from outlying villages and smaller towns: and there are often some who come from even further afield. These are the foreign students who come to take courses not available in their own countries: Saudi Arabians, Iraqis, Sheikhs' sons from Kuwait, people from Africa, Malaya, Thailand, Hong Kong—all places desperately in need of technologists of all kinds. Some come supported by grants from their governments, others are the sons and daughters of wealthy parents, and most of them work very hard.

It was about six years later, long after I had left the Reading area to settle in Aberystwyth, that I renewed my acquaintance with one of these students working so far away from home. I had driven my family to Swansea in order to do some shopping. During the afternoon we entered a large restaurant crowded with Saturday afternoon shoppers like ourselves.

Towards the end of our meal my wife noticed that a young man was obviously making his way to our table from a far corner of the room. Round to my side he came: 'Do you remember me?'

he said with a smile. 'I had to catch you before you went out'.
Here was one of a small group of Kuwaitis who had spent two
years at Reading Technical College before moving on to university. This particular one was spending further time at his oil
company's depot in South Wales before going back home, and
he had recognised me as I walked to my table. A chance meeting
that quite made my day.

My appointment in Reading had severed my close connections
with the Association of Assistant Librarians, so, when the annual
conference of the parent Library Association was announced I
applied for permission to attend it as a delegate, all expenses paid.

One year the conference was held in Llandudno, and there I
met for the first time a group of librarians from Eire, very keen,
but also excellent company. As a result, and much to my delight,
I was invited to deliver a paper the following winter at a meeting
of the Irish Library Association in Dublin: the City Librarian
of that wonderful city was keen to set up a college library in
their new technical college building, and she thought that it
would be of interest if I talked about the related problems I
had had to tackle.

At the suggestion of my hosts I extended my proposed visit
from one to four days by taking some leave. There followed the
most exciting time. From the moment of being met at the airport
to the time of my departure every minute of my stay was filled
with the most interesting things to see and fascinating people to
meet.

I was shown the sights of Dublin, the public buildings, the
museums and libraries, churches and monuments by the inde-
fatigable wife of an old colleague. I heard about the plans for a
modern extension to the great old library of Trinity College, and
I was able to examine their most famous treasure, the priceless
9th century Book of Kells, at leisure among friends and in
comfort.

How different it was from the first time I had gazed at this wonderful example of Celtic manuscript art and craftsmanship, as part of a long queue, in the presence of guards, when some of the Irish treasures had been loaned to the British Museum for a special exhibition. I also spent an hour or so in another great institution, the famous back room of Davy Byrne's pub.

The City Librarian herself continued the tour for me and, at the appointed hour, brought me—on the right side of a noble lunch—before my audience. My paper seemed a huge success. Everyone asked questions at the end, and there was none of the formal restraint of British audiences. The Irish are so enthusiastic: they work hard when they have to; they play hard with a clear conscience afterwards. That night there was the annual dinner of the conference, and the party that followed was a marvellous demonstration of how good a party can be.

I flew back home full of sadness at having to leave such a delightful country. We all had arranged to meet again at the next conference of the British Library Association—and we did.

Meanwhile, back in Reading, protracted negotiations were beginning to draw to a successful conclusion: the possibility of an extension to the college—and with it my new library—was nearer to becoming a reality. This was in 1962. I was told the basic area of floor space that had been allocated to the new library. It had been worked out according to a formula devised by the Ministry of Education, and now I had to prepare instructions for the architect so that he could design the interior to suit my needs.

Naturally I discussed my requirements and ideas for the layout with the Principal first of all. As far as I could, I embodied ideas which I had admired in other libraries of a similar nature, and I also provided a list of bad features which I was determined should be avoided.

Once our ideas had crystallised I drew a rough sketch plan to clarify my notes and provided clear explanations of the intended use of each different area of the library, as well as an estimate of

the number of volumes we expected it to hold. I also had to
state the size of reading desks we required for students to use in
the library, how far apart we wanted them, and how many were
required.

It may be wondered what work was being left for the architect.
In fact I was doing no more than any architect's client should do:
presenting a problem as clearly as possible.

To do this satisfactorily the librarian needs to have some
knowledge of matters such as work flow, lighting, shelving
capacities, or the amount of floor space taken up by one student
working at a desk. Without it his imagination will lead him to
produce instructions which the architect has no hope of following; with a sound brief the architect can then use his skill to
produce a building which is a tasteful and soundly constructed
embodiment of his client's wishes.

A week or two later the architect called in with his plans and
elevations to show his interpretation of our suggestions. He
had made a few rearrangements to utilise the space more effec-
tively; he wanted to know if these were acceptable or were
likely to cause future complications which he as a non-librarian
was unable to foresee. In fact he had interpreted our needs and
wishes very successfully: that was where we depended upon his
skill, and the revised layout gave us more storage and reading
space than we had dared to hope for.

The preparation of larger scale drawings could now begin, and,
in the meantime, we had to turn our thoughts towards the fittings.
What type of flooring ought we to specify? Wood block flooring,
though attractive, tends to be noisy in a library; cork tiles are
much more sound absorbent, but I knew that they are often
quick to wear and difficult to keep really clean.

Was there something more suitable? A new French resilient
plastic flooring had recently been tried out by some adventurous
local authorities. Was it as good as the manufacturers claimed?
The heating and lighting engineers joined the architect to discuss

their side of the project, and so our deliberations continued, as the weeks sped by.

The final plans were at last presented to the Board of Governors, and approved. Now it was the turn of the Ministry of Education to scrutinise them and the estimated cost of the building. Alterations were called for here and there; new drawings were made and again submitted for examination.

The tension grew, for every delay seemed to coincide with rising prices: the price of concrete went up, or the building industry secured a wage increase. Would approval be given only for us to discover that the final cost had rocketed above the amount we were allowed to spend? Then, one day, the good news arrived: we could go ahead with our plans and invite building firms to tender for the contract.

However, I never enjoyed the thrill of watching that new library grow out of the ground, and of eventually moving into it. Just before the builders arrived I saw another new post advertised by the Southampton College of Technology. They, too, had never had a college library or librarian before; a new building was in course of construction; they promised a larger staff than I had at Reading (with more staff I could provide a better library service and devote more time to the teaching of library usage). Moreover, and not the least of the attractions, they were offering a higher salary.

What a predicament to be in! I enjoyed living in the Thames Valley, with the delights of Sonning only twenty minutes' walk from home, and such places as Streatley, Marlow, Bisham, Henley, Hurley and Windsor dotted all around that lovely countryside. I enjoyed, too, my work at Reading, and there was the new library which I had planned with such pleasure.

Nevertheless, I also felt impelled to snatch at this unexpected opportunity of promotion, especially as I also liked the country around Southampton. After a certain amount of indecision I sent off my application: I had nothing much to lose either way.

A few weeks later I was on my way to another interview, and once more, after the committee had reached its decision, the name that was called out was mine. Could I start at Southampton on the 1st July 1963? 'I shall be delighted to', I said.

12

COLLEGE LIBRARY SERVICES ARE GROWING

THE NEW COLLEGE BUILDING at Southampton was in course of erection when I went for my interview. After the appointment had been approved by the Council and I had written my formal acceptance I was invited to meet the architect so that the fitting out of the library suite could be planned. At this stage the accommodation was little more than a bare concrete shell with the electric wiring dangling out of holes in the ceiling.

Certain aspects of the basic plan did not strike me as being good library design, but the building was too far advanced for any radical change to be made. As I got to know the architect better it became apparent that no one had considered the working problems of a college library when the original briefing had been prepared for him. However, we could still improve matters by concentrating upon a skilful arrangement of the shelving and counter areas.

I listed maximum and minimum sizes and distances for the various units, explained what tasks would be handled in the workroom, office and counter, and thus gave a clear picture of where bench high and where desk high working surfaces ought to be sited, and their relationship to the flow of work and users through the library. Back came the architect with variant designs of furniture and fittings, and together we were both convinced that we had achieved the best possible plan. The cabinet makers were now free to go ahead.

The planning and drawing of our fittings took far longer than it takes to tell. In my early days at Southampton I could not even share my quarters with the workmen, for the building was not ready to be handed over by the contractors. Accordingly I had to make do for a time in the corner of a storeroom, and then, when the summer vacation started, in an empty classroom.

My initial assessment of priorities at Reading had proved to be accurate enough in practice, so I did my basic ordering at Southampton with confidence based upon past experience. This time the apparent chaos was much less worrying to me.

One thing was different, however: I could look forward to a staff of three assistant librarians to help me just as soon as we could appoint them. This was one of the bonuses which had attracted me away from Reading. The posts had been advertised before my arrival; now we needed to call the most promising of the applicants for interview.

For the senior assistant I required a Chartered Librarian, male or female, who had had considerable experience in well-stocked libraries. I hoped to find someone who was used to reference work, at least, and who had perhaps even spent some time in a more junior post in another college library. I was also looking for someone with a personality which would appeal to students and staff alike, yet that someone had to be able to maintain discipline as well when I was not on duty. Ability on its own was not enough.

The two junior assistants had an even tougher situation to manage, in some ways. These two people, when found, might well be of the same age as the majority of our readers, yet, as staff of the college, they would need to maintain a friendly but businesslike relationship with everyone. It was also required of them that they should be capable of doing much of their work with the minimum of supervision because the library staff was still relatively low in numbers. Keenness and accuracy are essential additional qualities required of anyone interested in becoming a librarian.

During the month of September we moved into the new

building, and I was joined by my new staff. The new books began to arrive, the cataloguing and classifying got under way. Once again I was shaping the growth of a new library. For me it was a re-living of my early days at Reading: there were the same old doubts, the same old questions, but this time I could quote actual experience to substantiate my promises, and the fact that there were four of us at work in the library made it possible for more than one facet of the new service to be developed simultaneously.

There was one very big snag, however. This time not a single shelf was available in the very early days, even though the books were pouring in from the suppliers. Tables and desks for the new teaching accommodation were not due until late September, so there was only one thing to do: pile the books on the floor, and soon we had about £2,000 worth stacked in a corner.

I had never had to treat books like that before, and it all seemed very heartless, but circumstances were rather unusual for the moment, and we just had to be patient. When some of the lecture room furniture arrived I borrowed tables upon which we built up individual subject piles of books. The effect now was that of preparations for some gigantic bibliographical jumble sale, but I wanted to have a fair-sized initial collection to be completely ready to go on the shelves once they were fitted.

As with my previous new library there were decisions to make about which technical journals we ought to purchase. Most of the courses at Southampton were similar in content to those at Reading, but most colleges have one or two speciality courses connected with local industrial conditions. Southampton's importance as a port had resulted in the development of specialist courses in marine radar and radio, naval architecture and marine engineering. There were also plans to start courses in chemical engineering. In each case I had to study the syllabus and discuss it with the teaching staff so that I would know their needs too.

The remainder of my time—as at Reading in the early days—

was taken up with attending academic committees, meeting staff and making preparations for teaching programmes to include time for my contributions on the use of books and related library material, and because what I was doing was completely new to this college I again experienced the enjoyable stimulation of being a pioneer. With my staff fully entering into the spirit of the situation we had spent the initial grant of £5,000 for books long before the library was ready for opening.

When the time came for the preparation of estimates of expenditure for the next financial year I had to explain what the college plans for the future and its previous lack of library facilities meant in terms of an adequate book fund. I first had to convince the Principal; then he had in turn to convince the Board of Governors and the Chief Education Officer, whose task it would be to argue our case before the Education Committee.

From my early days as a college librarian I had found most informative the meetings organised by the Library Association sub-section for members in colleges of further education. The majority of those who met at these gatherings were relatively new to this type of work. A few who had pioneered in the field were glad to give valuable advice and encouragement, and the exchanges of experience were an important feature of the activities of this new sub-section.

In 1964 I was elected the Honorary Secretary, and later the same year the Library Association invited me to present a paper in a symposium on library service to students at its annual conference.

I was kept busy in other ways too. Since 1963 I had been an assistant examiner for the Library Association, and each summer and Christmas found me marking my share of examination scripts in my spare time. Many people tend to imagine that examiners are concerned only with failing candidates.

To join a team of examiners is often a revelation, therefore, because the reverse does in fact apply. Assistant examiners are carefully briefed as to how each answer should be marked; a standard marking scheme has to be followed; and, at the end, the chief examiner carefully inspects the marked scripts to ensure that personal variations have not crept into the allocation of marks.

Special attention is given to those candidates whose marks fall just below the pass level. Such borderline cases are reconsidered by the chief examiner, who checks over the marking to decide whether the answers deserve a slightly better mark or not in the light of the examiner's greater experience.

Within the College of Technology at Southampton the library continued to develop to everyone's satisfaction: the stock and the number of books issued increased as the months followed each other. The attractive décor, and the good working conditions made it a place in which students and staff found it easy to study. We were always included in the itinerary for important visitors to the college.

Outside the library I gradually made the acquaintance of neighbouring librarians from the public, university and special libraries in our area. I had done the same at Reading, for cooperation with one another opens up vast resources for the general benefit of all library users. An article in a periodical or a complete book may not be in one's own library stock—or it may be out on loan, but there may well be another copy which could be available within minutes of a telephone call to a friendly colleague four or five miles away.

Such co-operation in Hampshire eventually produced a suggestion from the City Librarian of Southampton that there should be a more tangible link between us all. The outcome of an exploratory meeting to discuss this was the setting up of the Hampshire Technical Research Industrial Commercial Service (HATRICS for short). A directory of all member libraries was compiled. This indicated the broad subject fields covered by each library's stock, the existence of any special collection they might have, and other useful information such as the name of the librarian.

The actual production of the directory up to the stage when it was ready for the printer was undertaken by a computer, to which one of our members had access.

Once the new co-operative scheme was operational a librarian whose own stock had failed to produce the answer to an enquiry could use the directory to check which other library in the area might be able to provide assistance, or the problem could be sent direct to the Central Reference Library at Southampton, which acted as a clearing house. Such local schemes exist in several parts of the country now, and they form a very speedy and useful supplement to the national interloan service, especially as far as technical information is concerned.

Within the bounds of my college there were also new developments: it had been decided to divide it into two specialising institutions, one for advanced work and the other for 'A' level and craft students. The advanced studies would be centred around the new buildings at East Park Terrace, and so their library service was already developing, but there were no parallel facilities in the older buildings about half a mile away which were to be redesignated eventually as a separate college of further education; and, up to this time, the students there had been encouraged to use the library at East Park Terrace.

Now, with the new library fairly well established, we could begin to set up a parallel library service on the old site. Although it would be regarded as a branch of the main library at first, it would have to be developed so that, eventually, it could serve in its own right as a separate library for the old college site when finally it became an independent unit.

Once more I was immersed in the intricacies of filling space with shelving, chairs and tables to best effect, aided on this occasion by the librarian whom we had chosen to take charge of the new branch library. After that, with an assistant to help her, and the resources of the main library to fall back upon when necessary, she was ready to embark upon the long process of building up her own stock.

In the October of 1965 a chance meeting at the Further Education Staff College produced a chain of events destined to induce me to move yet again. As a result of that meeting I was invited to give a special lecture on college librarianship to the students at the College of Librarianship Wales in Aberystwyth, and on a snowy Sunday in January 1966 I set off from my home in Winchester and pointed the car towards mid-Wales.

With a new engine that had yet to complete its running-in period I was forced to travel slowly though hopefully. Fortunately there was snow everywhere except upon the roads, as on I plodded for hour after hour. When I had left Herefordshire behind the solitude of the mountains closed around me, and even my passage through tiny hamlets did nothing to break the growing sense of isolation, for a Welsh Sunday in winter can make one feel that time itself has stopped.

Nevertheless, as I drove within sight of Plynlimon, Wales' second highest mountain, I also felt that I was entering a fairy-tale world, for the dark forests of fir trees were magically dusted with snow, and the frozen waterfalls and gigantic icicles hanging from the rocks presented a spectacle the like of which I had only seen in pictures.

The College itself completely fascinated me. Less than three years old, it was growing fast on a hillside just outside Aberystwyth. In front of it, on a hill across the valley, there were the concentric rings of an iron age fort, its summit crowned with an incongruous monument to Wellington, and its lower slopes spoiled by terraces of unimaginatively-arranged council houses. Between that hill and the next there was a glimpse of the sea.

The students were keen and friendly. Lecturing to them brought back the sense of challenge I had experienced when a visiting lecturer at the Manchester School of Librarianship. I realised that there was something more satisfying, as far as I was concerned, something more enjoyable, in this kind of teaching, than even college library work could offer.

The rest of my stay at Aberystwyth was a pleasant round of meetings with old acquaintances who were now on the staff of the college, visits to some of the libraries in the town, and even a tramp up the snow-covered slopes of Plynlimon. I stayed in a typical Welsh cottage, whitewashed and squat, hugging the ground as if to escape the winds that howled around its low roof at night. Inside we snuggled close around the fire, and I might have been a thousand miles away from Hampshire.

After my return from this visit it was plain that the experience had unsettled me. It was not the first time that I had felt strongly inclined to seek a post within a library school, but the opportunity had so far eluded me. When an advertisement appeared for posts at Aberystwyth shortly after my stay there I decided to regard it as an omen, and so I applied for one of the vacancies.

Within a few weeks I found myself being invited back to the college, this time for an interview. I was one of the successful applicants, and was asked to arrange to start my new duties as a senior lecturer in the following September—six months away. For that long waiting period I was extremely grateful: the longer I had in which to sell my house in Winchester and try to find another in the Aberystwyth area, the better.

13

LIBRARY SCHOOL:
TRAINING THE LIBRARIANS OF TOMORROW

My appointment at Aberystwyth was to lecture in book production, the history of printing and the literature and librarianship of chemistry.

Other members of the teaching staff specialise in different parts of the syllabus: library law and administration; cataloguing, classification and related aspects of information retrieval; bibliography; book illustration and binding; work with children; medical libraries; the presentation and dissemination of information; and the literature and librarianship of special collections in such fields as the fine arts, music, engineering, science, economics, English and Welsh literature. The full list is much longer.

The basic syllabus which has to be followed in preparation for the Library Association examinations, whether at non-graduate or post-graduate level, is an extensive one. Non-graduates, school leavers or those with one or two years' previous library experience, must have achieved five passes in the G.C.E., of which one must be in English language and two must be at Advanced level. In addition, the intending student must have reached a minimum standard of G.C.E. Ordinary level, or its equivalent, in a language other than English, or in a science. For such people there is a basic two-year course leading to Final examinations set by the Library Association.

Graduates follow a one-year course leading to an appropriate examination, again set by the Library Association, but, for these students, special course work projects are also taken into consideration during the final assessment of ability. Selection for a place in a library school is generally by personal interview long before the date of admission.

All except one of the British schools of librarianship have been created since the end of the Second World War. Fifteen in number, they are scattered up and down the country (two in Scotland, one in Northern Ireland, eleven in England, and one in Wales). Some are attached to universities, others are administered by local colleges of further education, and the single college in Wales is completely independent.

Some offer only post-graduate courses, others cater for the non-graduate as well. All have been set up to provide the country's library services with a steady flow of carefully schooled young entrants who have followed a recognised course of full-time study for one or two years. It is now accepted that part-time study does not allow for a sufficient broadening of the course.

In a library school the student has to make comparative studies of systems and procedures, arguing out conclusions in discussion with his fellows and the teaching staff. He hears talks by visiting speakers who are not necessarily librarians: binders, senior officials from the British Council, the Voluntary Service Overseas organisation, the Office for Scientific and Technical Information, representatives of the publishing world. The opportunity for question and answer that follows these talks is something that no one can obtain out of a textbook.

Those who have passed the Final or Post-graduate examination then qualify as a Chartered Librarian and become an Associate of the Library Association as soon as they have completed three years' work in an approved library. A library school course can count as one of these three, but one of them must also follow the passing of the examinations. Each school has its own approach to teaching, but I can only describe in detail my experience at the College of Librarianship Wales.

When I arrived at the College in the autumn of 1966 the long vacation was nearly over, but I had until October in which to

acquaint myself with the new surroundings and—even more
important—some time in which to start preparation of lecture
notes for the next academic year.

Oddly enough, when the winter term actually started, I was
missing from Aberystwyth, because I had a long-standing
invitation to act as Visiting Tutor for a week's conference on
college librarianship at the Further Education Staff College near
Bristol, and I had been given permission to continue with the
arrangement.

In October the students with no previous library experience
arrive at the College. As many as possible are allocated a place
in one or other of our hostels, and the rest move into rooms or
flats which have first been vetted by our Accommodation Officer.

All these students then take a special one-term Introductory
Course. There are general lectures on libraries and books, the
formal lectures being interspersed with seminars during which
the newly acquired information and previously conceived ideas
are used as the basis of discussion meetings in small groups of
eight or ten students led by one of the academic staff.

At the end of this programme there are six weeks of practical
work in a variety of libraries in selected large conurbation areas,
where the students are supervised both by the host librarians and
by touring lecturers from Aberystwyth. By Christmas, therefore,
both college and student have a fair idea of whether the intending
librarian is really suited to the course and to the profession.

The course leading to the Part 1 examination, which at
Aberystwyth and two other schools in England is an internal
examination, starts in January, when the students from the
Introductory Course are joined by those with some previous
library experience. No attempt is made to lecture to students
from morning to night: this is the big difference after school life.
About half of each working day is unscheduled on the timetable,
and the student is free to utilise this time as he pleases.

It may be that he prefers to have an afternoon off on the

beach or in the countryside, choosing to return to college in the evening to work in the library which does not close until 10 p.m. However he divides his day, the student must read and think about topics introduced to him during lecture periods, prepare written work for marking and collect information which will back up discussions and arguments in seminars.

From his first days in college he has a personal tutor to whom he may turn at any time for advice on personal or academic matters. I found that I had this special responsibility for about ten students, and on the first occasion upon which I met my tutorial group I had to admit that both sides were very much in the position of being newcomers.

For each of these students I had to keep a personal file, a record in fact of progress through the college: academic achievements, previous library experience if any, subsequent practical work experience, study tours undertaken, marks for written work and terminals, comments from the teaching staff, and even a photograph of the student, so that subsequent requests for, perhaps, a testimonial later on will be related to the achievements and personality of an individual.

The term leading up to Easter always seems to go very quickly, but before going down for the vacation there are important terminals. These examinations provide an indication of the amount of progress being made by each student, revealing strengths or weaknesses in the various subjects in good time for remedial action to be taken. During the actual vacation the college still claims some of the student's time: there are compulsory study tours of about one week's duration.

In groups of twenty-five, accompanied by two members of the teaching staff, there are organised visits to libraries of all kinds in carefully chosen areas. Some groups will visit Lancashire and Yorkshire, others will go to the Midlands, the Bristol area, South Wales or Hampshire. Accommodation is generally provided in student hostels in these areas, and care is taken to ensure that students visit areas as different as possible from their previous home background.

The purpose of these conurbation study tours is to provide a link and also a contrast between past experience, the studies undertaken during the first term and a number of real library situations. Students can ask practising librarians for their own views on lecture or textbook postulations, and real-life problems underline the validity of the classroom studies.

I was asked to lead one such tour to the Southampton-Winchester area, because I was familiar with the libraries there and knew many of the librarians. I could comment from practical experience upon what we should see, and there was no fear of our wasting precious time in getting lost en route from one library to the next. It was a rather strange sensation to take my party of visitors to the college of technology library where I had formerly been the librarian, but my successor asked me to join in as an extra guide, much to the amusement of the students.

Weeks of preparation go into making these tours as interesting and informative as possible: requests to visit this or that library are written to old friends, itineraries planned, coaches hired, hostels booked, off-duty evening concert or theatre parties arranged. However, the effort is not only on the part of the college staff. The hosts, the librarians we visit, busy though they may be, give up whole days to guide us around their libraries, treating the students as professional equals, outlining their hopes and fears, their successes and failures, and answering question after question. Spend a week doing this, and you will agree that we all earn the rest of the vacation!

The summer term starts and, before anyone realises it, the Part I examinations are upon us. The survivors go off on their own for another period of six weeks' practical work (in different types of library again, for variety), with a final study tour—of London libraries—to follow during the next Easter vacation.

It may come as a surprise that so many tour and practical work

periods are considered essential at Aberystwyth. Students themselves are apt to comment at first, 'Surely one library is very
much like another?' This reaction passes, however, the more the
student sees and learns. He moves from the world of municipal
and county libraries to university or college; from the industrial
library within an internationally famous firm to government and
national research establishments. All have their own problems,
their different approaches to book selection, their own ways of
organisation and administration.

Another summer vacation activity at Aberystwyth, for post-
graduate and second-year non-graduate students alike, is the
overseas study tour. It is not enough for our students to know
what is going on in British libraries: we want them to compare
notes with the staffs of important libraries on the Continent and in
Scandinavia. We also want to go ourselves, for we must never
stop learning. The design of some modern equipment and of
recent new library buildings in several parts of Britain has been
influenced by what British librarians have seen during visits
abroad since the end of the Second World War.

So many of our students go abroad each summer that several
tours have to be arranged by the teaching staff, Holland,
Germany, Denmark and Sweden being our main goals, but a
large party has also visited the United States. My experience as
joint leader of a two-week tour of Swedish libraries may be
taken as typical.

Months before the date of our tour initial plans had been drawn
up: which library systems did we wish to visit, which could we
possibly reach within the limits of time and foreign currency
allowances? How many visits ought we to make without running
the risk of seeing so much that we became mentally unable to
absorb any more facts and figures? Carefully planned free time
not only makes some sightseeing possible, but also refreshes the
mind for further library visits: in other words, 'All work and
no play . . .'

In these early days of planning the experience of staff members who had led previous tours was carefully taken into account: will we need to hire taxis to get to our hotel in Stockholm, or can we manage on buses? Were last year's hotels good enough without being too expensive? And so on.

There still remained the task of writing to each Librarian whose services we wished to see to ask if indeed we might make the visit. As a result the itinerary had to be changed here and there to fit in with other commitments of our hosts, or a proposed afternoon visit changed to the morning because someone wished to entertain us all to lunch as well as to show us round their library.

Eventually it was possible to give those students who had chosen our tour a fairly accurate cost figure for the two weeks we should be away, final reservations on planes, trains and coaches were made, and insurance against loss of baggage, accidents and illness was taken out for each member of the party. Nothing was left to chance.

On the day of our departure we all met at Gatwick airport and joined Danish and Swedish students who were returning home on our flight to Copenhagen after visits to Britain. By early evening we were ready to explore the Danish capital. At that time of day, in the summer, many Danes go to the Tivoli gardens, and so did we. The next day, Saturday, was free, and in two's and three's we continued our explorations. Some went shopping for presents and souvenirs; some preferred to enjoy the glorious sunshine from the coolness of the old canals of the city, and went sightseeing by boat.

Early next morning we took the ferry to Malmö, arriving there just after lunch, again with time in hand to see something of the town before dusk. Starting on the Monday we visited numerous libraries, national, public, university and technical, in places as far apart as Malmö, Gothenburg, Lund, Stockholm and Uppsala. Swedish children are very fond of puppets, it seems, and several libraries we saw had special story rooms where the children gather to act out stories or just to sit and listen to stories being told by the children's librarian. In Gothenburg's beautiful Central Library we sat in a special section of their music department, each one of us listening to a record of our own choice through stereo headphones.

We went back in the evening and there was a queue of people awaiting their turn. If we had lived there we could also have borrowed records to take home, just as one can in some British libraries, but it was the luxury and comfort of the furnishings, and the quality and quantity of the equipment that opened our eyes to Scandinavian standards.

In technical and medical libraries we talked about mutual problems in making literature searches by computer. In the university libraries of Lund and Uppsala, as well as being shown round their buildings we saw some of their great treasures, including the Codex Argenteus, a Gothic version of the Four Gospels written on leaves of purple-dyed parchment to show off the silver ink. We compared library design of the 1930's with the latest libraries of the 1960's. We met representatives of the Swedish Library Inspectorate, and fittingly, our tour ended with a visit to the Royal Library in Stockholm.

Our off-duty moments were equally crowded: one particularly remembers the Götaplatsen and Carl Milles' Poseidon fountain in Gothenburg; the old city hall in Copenhagen, and the very modern one in Stockholm, both equally beautiful in their own way; an afternoon in the 18th century theatre and gardens of Drottningholm; cathedrals at Lund and Uppsala; the great buildings and magnificent vistas of Stockholm.

Stockholm deserves a book to itself: no wonder it is called the Venice of the North. By night or day, in the old town or the new, we all fell in love with that wonderful city by the water. The Swedes' pleasure in the sight of moving water is exemplified by the delightful fountains in many parks and public squares.

For those who had not been abroad before there were also the added thrills of strange sights and sounds. Even buses, trains and trams are different in another country, and of course there was the fun of trying to make oneself understood (though so many people over there speak very good English), or wrestling with a foreign currency.

Also during the second year there are specially arranged three-day courses for those who are specialising in certain parts of the syllabus. Small groups set off to make a detailed study of hospital or technical libraries. Another group, with attendant lecturers, have a special interest in the history of book production, and the Gregynog weekend course in Print Handling and Binding has already become something of a legend.

Gregynog Hall, in Montgomeryshire, is now a Conference Centre for the University of Wales. During the first half of this century it was a privately-owned mansion and the home of the Gregynog Press, whose books, beautifully illustrated and printed and bound by hand in limited editions now fetch very high prices among collectors of fine books. In the old print shop our students actually set type by hand and print from it on an old hand press. They experience for themselves the difficulties and skills required to produce even a simple broadsheet. Then they visit the bindery upstairs to see the various stages in binding books by hand being demonstrated by a former member of the Gregynog Bindery staff.

In the evenings there might be a lecture on the history and significance of the Press within the British private press movement; the former Secretary of the Gregynog Press comes to reminisce about the printers and illustrators who designed and made the books, handing round copies to illustrate her points as she talks; or else a National Book League exhibition of modern fine printing from the commercial world will be on display for examination and comment.

The student who looks hard and listens intently during these and similar excursions from the college is amassing the fruits of a life-time's experience. When he takes his Final examination he can quote not only from theory but also from practice.

The post-graduate one-year course follows a very similar pattern, but the effort required is more intense because there is less time available. Practical course work set by the tutors is designed to supplement lectures and discussions, and it also links up with the special subject knowledge acquired during the earlier university course. This work is assessed upon completion, and supports the formal examination results at the end of the year.

Of course the student who works hard should also find time to enjoy some of the social advantages of college life, and library school students at Aberystwyth have the benefit not only of their own events but also of the university students' union activities. There are dances and socials; posters outside the common room exhort readers to attend Film Society performances, to join a Chess Club or to take part in debates; there is an announcement about a ramble through the upper Ystwyth valley, or a more protracted excursion to the top of Snowdon. There are car rallies, football and cricket matches in due season, with badminton and the use of an indoor swimming pool if it rains.

A library school is always deeply concerned about the future of libraries and the library profession. The last few years have seen a great deal of discussion about educational plans for tomorrow. Some schools are now able to offer courses leading to C.N.A.A. (Council for National Academic Awards) degrees; others offer a university diploma or degree course.

As from 1968 my own college, in conjunction with University College, Aberystwyth, has pioneered a joint honours degree of the University of Wales, and this is attracting students who wish to study both academic subjects and librarianship at degree level. Such courses are slightly longer than those already described, and the academic content is taught within University College.

This development is a sign of the times: tomorrow's librarian will be expected to possess a better all-round education than ever before, and already we are finding that a more mature and perceptive type of student is seeking admission to our college because of this new approach to professional education.

In the last few years the staffs of the library schools have made considerable impact upon many aspects of librarianship outside the field of education. Lecturers are not expected to spend all their time in the classroom, but are encouraged to undertake research. Some of these projects are financed by government grants received through such agencies as the Office of Scientific and Technical Information; others are undertaken privately out of personal interest.

The results may be published as articles in the professional journals, or there may be enough material for a book. A number of new books for students of librarianship have appeared recently as by-products of this teaching experience. We cannot afford to become dry academics, completely out of touch with day-to-day librarianship, and so far there is no sign that this is likely to happen: our commitment to our profession is deep and our ties with practising librarians too strong.

In retrospect it has been the variety of experience within librarianship that has appealed to me as much as the type of work itself. Now, more than ever before, there is a growing opportunity 'to get out and take librarianship to the public: to take it into the schools, the factories, the organised groups and societies, even, in some cases, into the homes of the public. And not only to take it there, but to make it obviously relevant and necessary there'. Those words were spoken by R. J. Edwards, Liaison and Training Officer in the College of Librarianship Wales, during the course of a paper delivered at the Library Association's 1968 Public Libraries Conference at Brighton. His list of areas needing library services should be extended to include colleges, universities, hospitals and government departments.

Certainly, for those who look for them, there are ample opportunities to change the direction of one's professional life, and, now and again, there are also unexpected turns to add excitement. A colleague at college has just been invited by the British Council to go to Malaysia for two years as a Library Adviser, and I am looking forward to a year's leave of absence to undertake research for a higher degree. With some twenty years to go before I retire, I wonder what lies ahead?

APPENDIX

If you wish to know more about education for librarianship you should write to *The Library Association, 7 Ridgmount Street, Store Street, London WC1.*

The Library Association publishes a *Students' Handbook*, which includes the addresses of all the different library schools in Britain, and each school publishes a prospectus giving full details of its courses and admission requirements.

Application for admission to any library school should be made as early as possible, even before 'A' level examinations are taken. Otherwise you may find that all the places are already filled.